*Astrology and
Heredity*

Astrology and Heredity

The Thread of Life

ROSEMARY PEEL

BLANDFORD

DEDICATION

To my husband, the non-believer, without whose encouragement this book would never have been completed.

To my long-suffering family for putting up with me.

To the McLernans – past, present and to come, wherever they may be. I'm proud to be one of 'The Clan'.

A Blandford Book

First published in the UK by Blandford
A Cassell Imprint
Cassell Plc, Villiers House
41/47 Strand, London WC2N 5JE

Copyright © 1994 Rosemary Peel

Distributed in the United States by Sterling Publishing Co., Inc., 387 Park Avenue South, New York, NY 10016-8810

Distributed in Australia by Capricorn Link (Australia) Pty Ltd, 2/13 Carrington Road, Castle Hill, NSW 2154

British Library Cataloguing-in-Publication Data
A catalogue entry for this title is available from the British Library

ISBN 0-7137-2477-3

Typeset by Litho Link Limited, Welshpool, Powys

Printed and bound in Finland by Werner Söderström Oy

Contents

Preface

It is the intention of the author that this book should be of interest to both the established astrologer and to the student or, in fact, anyone who has an interest in the subject. This work neither contains information on how to construct a birth chart, nor any relevant tables for doing so. There are, at the present time, plenty of books on the market which contain both. A birth chart can, of course, be obtained from a professional astrologer at any time.

Nevertheless, because the reader must understand the basic principles of astrology before attempting the later chapters on hereditary patterns, I will begin with a general introduction.

Introduction

Before I start, I should like to apologize for the constant referral to my own and my family's astrological placings within this book. The reason for using members of my family as examples, rather than well-known personalities, is because firstly, I am reasonably sure that the interpretations of the placings are accurate. Secondly, most of the data for my research has come from my own family (and from people closely connected to it). The maternal side of my family is Scottish and since the Scots have the good sense to include the time of birth on the birth certificate, my job has been made easier. I should ask, therefore, the indulgence of the reader for the personal slant of this book and for my part, I promise to do my utmost to keep the text interesting.

Most people are aware of their sun signs and the popular horoscope feature in newspapers and magazines will bear this out. But this is only a small part of the complete picture. Nevertheless, because of the familiarity of the sun signs, it is a useful place to start.

All the signs are involved in a birth chart. It is their dispersal through the 360° of the zodiac and the specific placings of the planets (and personal points) within them that make an astrological birth chart totally unique. There are 12 signs of the zodiac, beginning with Aries and following through to Pisces. These 12 signs are divided up into several groups. Let us take a closer look at the signs through these different divisions.

Division by six gives two groups of six signs; the positive (or masculine) and the negative (or feminine) ones. The terms positive and negative are not intended to be interpreted as strong and weak, or good and bad; nor are the terms masculine and feminine intended to be used in their sexist sense. Both these terms simply indicate that the positive signs are active in nature whilst the negative ones are passive.

Positive Signs	Negative Signs
Aries	Taurus
Gemini	Cancer
Leo	Virgo
Libra	Scorpio
Sagittarius	Capricorn
Aquarius	Pisces

The signs alternate between positive and negative.

Division by three gives four groups of three signs. This groupage is called 'the elements'. There are three signs in each of the four elements (fire, earth, air and water). The fire signs are warm, forceful personalities, who have an inborn need to be noticed and out in front. The earth signs are quiet, cautious and practically minded with a need for security. The air signs which are versatile and intellectually inclined have a need to communicate. The water signs are emotionally motivated and fluctuating by nature and their need is for emotional security.

Fire	Earth	Air	Water
Aries	Taurus	Gemini	Cancer
Leo	Virgo	Libra	Scorpio
Sagittarius	Capricorn	Aquarius	Pisces

Note: The fire and air signs are positive, whilst earth and water are negative.

A further division by four, gives three groups of four signs. These are called 'the qualities'. They are: cardinal, fixed, and mutable. Cardinal signs are initiators, driving-force personalities. These people are ambitious. Even in the natural world cardinal signs begin new phases, the first degree of each beginning a new season of the year. The fixed signs are steady, solid characters, fixed in nature and opinion. If you want reliability and constancy, then look no further. The mutable signs, by contrast, are restless and changeable. Variety is a necessity for them or their highly-strung nerves begin to show signs of strain.

Cardinal	Fixed	Mutable
Aries	Taurus	Gemini
Cancer	Leo	Virgo
Libra	Scorpio	Sagittarius
Capricorn	Aquarius	Pisces

There is yet another division, this time by two, giving six signs of two polarities (or opposites). Polarities provide the balance required by nature, wherein two halves make up one whole. They are important and should not be under-estimated. Each sign is opposed by its polarity yet has a lesson to learn from it. One needs and draws from the other. For example, the tendency of Aries to go it alone becomes, in Libra, a need to share with others, but the basic tendency to want to 'do it my way' remains.

Libra really would 'like to teach the world to sing in perfect harmony' – just so long as it can be composer, lyricist and conductor!

The Polarities

Aries	–	Libra
Taurus	–	Scorpio
Gemini	–	Sagittarius
Cancer	–	Capricorn
Leo	–	Aquarius
Virgo	–	Pisces

This then is the make-up of the signs. In the next chapter we will look at them individually.

Chapter 1

The First Six Signs:
Aries to Virgo

In the following passages the signs are treated as entities in themselves – which, of course, they are not. It should be remembered that it is the mixture of all the signs involved in a birth chart that represents the individual, and not merely the sun–sign characteristics.

✍ Aries

Brave scarlet dreams by impulse fed,
The soldier and the poet, dwell side by side,
By Mars they're ruled and cannot help but show it.

Aries is the first sign of the zodiac. It begins each year when the sun reaches the Equator at the spring equinox. Its mix is positive, fire and cardinal. Its polarity is Libra (the sign that occurs as the sun returns to the Equator and brings about autumn). The nature of Aries is very basic – like the new-born infant, it sees and feels its own needs and lets you know, in no uncertain terms, if it doesn't get what it wants. People with a strong Aries content in their chart tend to be self-orientated.

Aries has a simplistic way of looking at the world. Things are either right or wrong, good or bad. Grey areas do not exist. It cannot – or will not – acknowledge their existence. This is the sign of the pioneer, willing and able to go it alone. It is also the sign of the general who leads his troops from the front – head first, so to speak. It was probably an Arien who ordered (or at least led) the Charge of the Light Brigade! It is impulsive by nature, ready to charge into hell – if it is to its own benefit to do so. The strange thing is that somehow Aries generally manages to succeed in reaching the unreachable.

Aries is a survivor. One that may get a little battered along the way – but survives none the less, often to repeat the same mistakes all over again! It is a sign of impossible dreams, always just out of reach, and yet it is willing to spend a whole lifetime striving to attain them. The eternal optimist – that's Aries!

Although a somewhat selfish sign, it is never intentionally so. There is so much warmth about Aries and such enthusiasm that people generally overlook, or forgive, such failings. Even its temper – which is exceedingly short-fused – comes as lightning flashes. Anger is gone as quickly as it arrives and it harbours no malice. Brooding moodiness is simply not in its nature.

Life for Aries is a fast and furious ride on a magical merry-go-round – exciting, exhilarating and enjoyable – if you can stand the pace.

♉ Taurus

Strong but gentle sons of earth
At one with Nature's world, and deep beneath
The stubborn streak Venusian love's unfurled.

Taurus, the second sign of the zodiac, is negative, earth, and fixed in make-up. This sign, the earthiest of the earth group, deliberately and forcefully, digs its roots into nature's bountiful resources. There is a purposeful strength and a deep sense of belonging about Taurus that make people naturally turn to it for support and encouragement. Practical and reliable – the working cart-horse as opposed to the dainty thoroughbred. If ever there was a sign made to move mountains – stone by steady stone – it's this one. Not that Taurus would want to move anything. Change in essence upsets it. The way things were, the way things are, that's the way they should remain – this is Taurean philosophy, which leads to its greatest fault: an unwillingness to accept new ideas or new surroundings (or even new people). Ruts are comfortable and Taurus loves comfort, which in turn is part and parcel of its famed stubborn nature. Stubbornness and obstinacy are inadequate words to describe this side of the Taurean character. Bloody-minded, cut off your nose to spite your face, obduracy is nearer the mark. Not that Taurus sees it that way. Far from it. Constancy, determination, perseverance – that's the bull's terminology. Don't you believe it!

But I suppose it can no more help this side of its nature than Aries can help being selfish, and we so readily forgive the ram! It is just that Taurean stubbornness is far more difficult to deal with and intensely irritating to more flexible beings. You can appeal to Aries, point out that it is being self-centred – and it is quite likely to agree with you. But with Taurus, you may as well talk to the wall – you'd be far more likely to get a positive response!

That aside, its good points do outweigh its bad. Taurus is an earthy romantic with a solid practicality and a physically sensuous nature. It has a natural appreciation of beauty, art and music. Indeed, all of life's little luxuries appeal to it and it does seem to have the knack of being able to make the money needed to purchase them. Taurus likes to own its own home, car, caravan, land, video, television – you name it, Taurus wants to own it. Oh, and by the way, it also tends to try and own people too!

Possessiveness is an intrinsic part of its make-up. This leads to a jealous streak – another difficult characteristic. It is a combination of the possessive and jealous instincts that cause its normally placid temper to blow – and when it does, *Boy! Does it blow!* Blind fury, is the term that comes to mind. As far as this sign is concerned, I really do know what I'm talking about, from both angles. I am by sun sign a Taurean myself and I am also married to one.

Life for Taurus is a comfortable, steady stroll around the world of bountiful nature – with which, above all other signs, it is indeed totally in tune.

♊ Gemini

Sweet mystery of multitude;
Imagine if you can, the myriad complexities
Of this Mercurial man.

Gemini, the third sign of the zodiac, is a positive, air and mutable mixture. Gemini is an intelligent, restless sign. Information is its life-blood. Not necessarily academic knowledge – just everything about everything. It is a butterfly of a sign and needs to fly unrestrained, picking up what information it can along the way and then passing on that information to anyone who cares to listen. It thrives on communication.

Gemini is probably one of the best signs to have in a chart in conjunction with other more dependable and serious signs. It adds quickness of intellect, manual dexterity and an unerring and unbiased logic. It does, however, need the steadying influence of earth and the emotional depth of water to function at its best. For, like all good things, too much is a recipe for disaster – or at least a criminal waste of God-given talents.

The insatiable curiosity that is Gemini, is both a blessing and a curse. Whilst its active mind never tires of learning, or gaining (and maintaining for ever-ready access), unlimited knowledge and information, the means can become an end in itself. The wealth of stored information, combined with communicative skills, gives the ability to converse intelligently (and with great verbosity) on just about any subject you care to mention. The trouble is that Gemini tends to be satisfied with knowledge for its own sake and does not apply it to any practical purpose. Thus, its marvellous mentality, can degenerate into an intellectual attic, cluttered with mounds and mounds of useless information. What a pity!

The gifts that this sign has been endowed with are great indeed: a quick-silver mentality; a thirst for knowledge; great communicative skills; fingers as dextrous as the mind is active and on top of that a supple, ever-youthful, physical body! *Why are such gifts so often wasted on the superficial accumulation of mindless trivia?*

You may think that I am being too hard in my assessment of

the twins. The problem is, that I find it very difficult to be detached when it comes to the third sign of the zodiac. Both my parents are sun-sign Geminians and, as you can imagine, I have it very strongly in my own make-up. It is only through my astrological studies that I have come to acknowledge and attempt to deal with the above tendencies within myself – and believe me, it is a constant struggle.

When this sign predominates a chart, the interests can become so diverse that they fragment altogether. I constantly thank heaven for the strong Taurus content in three out of four of my grandparents, which I am sure, induced my birth to precede its expected date by a whole month – otherwise I would have arrived when the sun, too, was in Gemini!

To conclude: if life for Aries is a merry spin, for Gemini it is a supersonic flight, viewed with kaleidoscopic vision! Is it any wonder, then, that it is loath to land – even to recharge its highly-strong nerves – let alone allow time for anything or anybody to curtail its happy wanderings?

◀ Cancer

Forever bathed in pale moonlight
Emotions ebb and flow, unfathomed depths
Of feelings rare, that few will ever know.

Cancer's mix is negative, water and cardinal. Don't ever take this sign at face value, for it is never what it seems. Like all cardinal signs, it is an ambitious go-getter, unwilling simply to sit and wait for things to happen but ready and able to initiate the first move. Cancer tends to do this in a roundabout manner. Directness is never its strategy, but it does know what it wants in life and, more often than not, succeeds in achieving it – at least on a practical level. (Emotionally? Well, that's another matter.)

The first day of Cancer coincides with the arrival of summer, as the sun reaches the Tropic of Cancer. There is indeed the warmth of summer in the emotional depths of this complex sign. But, like its symbol, the crab, Cancer hides not only its vulnerable soft centre within its crusty exterior, but also the genuine affection of its loving nature. The inner self is indeed ultra-soft, super-sensitive and very vulnerable, so the safety precaution of the outer shell is necessary. The trouble is, that sometimes it is only this crusty exterior that is seen and the crab is totally misunderstood, which hurts! Its answer is to retreat still further into its shell, until there is nothing of the gentler side of its nature left showing! It is a vicious circle – and one that takes some resolving for the crab itself. Much patience and understanding is needed from those who come into close contact with it and have to contend with its constantly changing moods.

Cancer is a nurturing sign in both the sexes. The need to care for and protect are paramount. It is tenacious in holding on to what is important to it, and thus, it is often accused of being tight-fisted. This is another injustice. To have, is simply to hold on to. This is Cancer's philosophy and it applies it to people as well as inanimate objects. Cancer needs to be able to see and touch the things it values most. This comes from an inner need for constant reassurance as Cancer's highly emotional nature is very insecure. Cancerian parents often suffer tremendous pain when children leave their protective care.

Letting go is very difficult for Cancer. Not that it will show it – far from it! The anguish and hurt will be stored, deep inside, away from prying eyes, but there it will be nurtured until it tears at the very heart-strings. What's more, these self-inflicted wounds will constantly reopen whenever tender memories come flooding back.

Life for Cancer is an ebb and flow of sensitive responses. Instincts are strong and deep. Relationships – for better or worse – are made to last. It is a journey across the unfathomable oceans of emotional experience.

♌ Leo

A brave heart filled with Summer's Sun,
Of metal purest gold;
The monarch in his finery, resplendent to behold.

Positive, fire, fixed is the Leo mixture. Leo is the second of the fire signs but here, the fires of Aries are tempered by combination with the fixed quality. Where Aries is hot, Leo is warm – wonderfully warm. It oozes from its extrovert personality, to such an extent that you can almost physically feel it. There is a reassuring air of confidence about Leo that other people automatically notice.

This is a proud and forceful sign, brimming with self-confidence and self-worth. Organization on a grand scale is its speciality – mind you it will leave some other poor soul to do the clearing up. The lion loves to shine and tends to hug the limelight. Therein lies its weakness. Because it loves to be admired and looked up to, it easily falls prey to flattery. It is so easy to flatter Leo. It falls for it every time! This is probably because this is how Leo sees itself, mirrored in an image of splendour, benevolence and greatness. Shame it doesn't always live up to the image!

Leo is strong and brave, and almost as fixed in its opinions as Taurus (almost, but not quite). Make no mistake about it, it is very capable. The trouble is that Leo tends to dramatize everything, even itself. It sees the world in larger than life terms. The dreams it dreams, like everything about it, are on a grand scale. Defeat or failure doesn't enter into its reckoning, so that when, on occasion, life hits it in the face, it falls harder than most.

Leo is so rarely down that when it is, it can find it very difficult to swallow that all-consuming pride and admit that it needs help. On these occasions, it is up to those around it to give the required help in the most unobtrusive way possible. Not too much to ask, to save the Leo self-esteem, is it?

Leo is in essence a generous spirit combined with a lovingly warm personality. It has its foibles, one of which is a jealous streak that can be every bit as difficult to handle as that of Taurus. But, above all, it has the wonderful talent of entertainment (in private as well as in public) and one of the greatest gifts of all – that of being able to make people laugh. Mind you, remember to laugh with a Leo, not at it, or the teeth, claws and fearsome roar of the King of the Beasts will manifest – it would have to be 'The King', wouldn't it!

The proof of the warmth of Leo, if any were needed, was personally brought home to me through the demise of two very special Leo ladies (my mother-in-law and a very dear aunt). The world is noticeably colder and emptier without them. I cannot think of this sign without bringing to mind fond and loving memories of these generous-natured and affectionate ladies.

Life for Leo, very simply, is for living. It is fun; a playful romp, which it generously wishes to share with pleasant companions. The warmth of summer sunshine permeates its extrovert personality, and makes the world a pleasanter place in which to live.

♍ Virgo

Mercurial thoughts feed high strung nerves,
Belied by calm, clear eyes; misunderstood,
The Virgo heart can't help but criticize.

Virgo is possibly the most difficult sign of all to understand and, thus, so often it is the most misunderstood. It is a negative, earth sign but its quality is mutable. This in itself is hard to understand: how can solid earth be mutable? The shifting sands of desert regions or the unstable terrain of earthquake belts come to mind? This, is Virgo: at its best, shifting sands of finely tuned nerves; at its worst, a potential for cataclysmic disaster!

Virgo makes life difficult for itself. It wants perfection, but unfortunately, this is an imperfect world. The trouble is, it finds it almost impossible to settle for anything less. It applies this harsh criteria not only to itself, but also to everything (and everybody) with whom it comes in contact. It is constantly dissatisfied with its own efforts and looks to better things in others – but again is destined for disappointment! Thus, it becomes disillusioned and unhappy.

The preconceived idea of this sign as neat and tidy, highly domesticated, and pristine, with a permanent eye on health and hygiene, is far too limited for this complex sign. True, there are very health-conscious Virgos, and those who are almost obsessive about personal and domestic hygiene. Although, I know some very untidy, highly undomesticated and even downright disorganized Virgos!

This stereotype is only one form of expression for the analytical nature of the sign. It is concerned with – no, obsessed by – details. No matter what it does or is interested in, it is the minute and often (to other people) unimportant aspects that assume priority. This is what gives it its over-fussy ways. It is as if Virgo was put here to attend to the finer points; the small print, in life's contract.

The other intrinsic part of its character is its critical outlook. Because of an inborn need to get to the bottom of things, it seems to have acquired an instinctive shrewdness. This has nothing to do with the intuitive nature of its polarity, Pisces, but sometimes it works in a similar manner. It has an uncanny knack of seeing through people, and this can be very off-putting. Possibly because of this ability, Virgo tends to put up a barrier around itself. It can go through life without ever allowing another human being to see beyond this safety zone.

I have a sneaking feeling that Virgo doesn't care for what is hidden inside. This sign is very deep. Contrarily, it is almost Scorpionic in its ability to delve into the souls of others, while keeping its own dark secrets.

Part of the reason Virgo puts up its emotional barrier is because it tries to avoid the pain of emotional experience. As a child it soon learns that to become attached to something – be it a toy or a pet, or a person – can lead to pain when that object is taken away. It reasons, quite logically, that if it doesn't allow itself to get involved emotionally, then it will not have to suffer the pain of bereavement or loss.

This deliberate withdrawal of emotional response continues into adolescence. Only once will Virgo be hurt by romantic rejection, after that the barrier goes up and never again will anyone be allowed close enough to inflict pain. Perhaps this is why there are so many bachelors and spinsters (and lonely old people) with this sign strong in their make-up. Perhaps this is why Virgo so often throws itself whole-heartedly into its work – as compensation? I wonder.

I would add that this self-inflicted emotional isolation is mitigated if the sign is mixed with water and/or fire signs. If, however, it is mixed with the other earth signs, this tends to exacerbate the situation, giving an exaggerated need for material and monetary acquisitions.

As I said at the start, Virgo is a very difficult sign to understand. I don't think it ever really understands itself. Life for Virgo is a hard and sustained struggle in a world of harsh realities. It is a sad irony that this sign, which has an inner need for affection and love, somehow doesn't have the ability to communicate the fact.

Virgo is the last of the so-called personal signs (the first six signs of the zodiac). Their polarities, Libra to Pisces, often called the impersonal ones, will be looked at in detail in the next chapter.

Chapter 2

The Second Six:
Libra to Pisces

♎ Libra

In search of beauty, peace and love, go Libra
Sons and daughters. From Venus comes the oil they pour
Upon life's stormy waters.

Libra is another highly stereotyped sign. It is second only to
Virgo in being misinterpreted. The general view is that Libra
is all sweetness and light, being gentle, caring, and indecisive
by nature and totally reliant on other people. Sorry, but no it
isn't! Libra's mix is positive, air and cardinal. It also has Aries
as its polarity. Does that sound a weak, shilly-shallying
combination? Certainly not!

It is true that Libra dislikes disharmony and will avoid
confrontation if it can. But that is not to say that it can be
walked upon. No, rather it manipulates, in the nicest possible
way, of course. Co-operation is what it seeks, but more often
than not it is other people who have to do the co-operating.

The cardinal quality added to the air element sometimes
masks itself in a Leonian type of personality. Libra likes the
sound of its own voice, and it can certainly talk! Wherever you
hear the buzz of conversation, the one taking centre-stage will
either be a Leo or a Libra, you can bet on it! Oh, I know
Sagittarius likes to be noticed, but that is a more physical
domination. Libra's is verbal and intellectual (it is an air sign).

The logic of Libra is impeccable. Don't try and outdebate it:
you can't! Only Gemini could give it a run for its money, if it
had the inclination, but there are too many distractions to hold
Gemini's attention for long enough. The trouble with Libra,
despite the fact that it likes peace and quiet, is that it simply
can't avoid arguing. What it finds hard to understand is that

other people sometimes get heated when arguments go against them. Libra is perfectly capable of a cool, detached, logical debate, and it is well equipped for it. Unfortunately, it is often the instigator of full-scale rows but never intends things to get out of hand. It simply states its point of view, highlights the injustices, etc. and really doesn't understand why people suddenly turn nasty. Oh dear! Poor Libra.

'It's not fair!' is its frequent cry. No, it's not! Like the Virgo quest for perfection, Libra's thirst for fairness and justice, in a very unfair and unjust world, is doomed to failure. But Libra, unlike Virgo, is always willing to give it another try (Aries optimism perhaps?). It takes the same attitude to people. Optimistically it believes each time that this one will be perfect.

Libra does need people. Lonely Libra is a desolate sight. But this is not to lean or depend upon. It is simply to be with; to share the ups and downs of life. It does have a downright romantic side to its make-up; but this tends to have a materialistic base. Romantic settings for Libra are usually expensive ones, and love on a budget is not likely to appeal to its extravagant nature. Love will very quickly fly out of the window if it is required to live in squalor – it simply can't put up with it. If the love of your life is a Libra, I suggest you check your bank balance before rushing headlong into a permanent relationship or it could end up anything but permanent.

Life for Libra is a search for beautiful things; for beautiful people; harmonious relationships, and peaceful surroundings. In fact, a quest for Paradise! In a world such as this, it surely needs all the strength of character is possesses, coupled with an optimistic outlook (from Aries) to remain undaunted in the face of such odds against success.

♏ Scorpio

The highest heights; the lowest depths
In Pluto's realm are found; intensified emotions,
To conquer or be drowned.

As has been repeatedly stated in many astrological works,

Scorpio has a sting, but it also has some very endearing qualities. Not the least of which is its loyalty and devotion to family and friends. Scorpio is a fixed, negative, water sign. It has a great deal in common with its polarity, Taurus. Both have great strength and determination. Both are possessive and jealous. Both are steadfast, loyal and true. But the motivation for Scorpio is emotional.

There has been a lot of drivel written about this sign. What I am talking about is the constant referral to sex and the sex drive in connection with the eighth sign of the zodiac. Sure, to a certain extent this is a sexy sign – but no more than is Taurus, or Leo, or even Pisces for that matter. What apparently makes the difference, or at least makes it more noticeable in Scorpio, is what sets it apart from all other signs – its intensity.

This is a sign of extremes; of an all-or-nothing approach to life. Scorpio can't help it. This is what gives it such a powerful energy source. Like the power in a lightning bolt, you can see it; you can feel it, almost *before* you see it – but you can't harness it! This is Scorpio, for better or worse.

Scorpio is a powerful sign and the power shines through its rather introverted personality as a kind of magnetic force. It is a strange kind of magnetism; one that attracts and repels at the same time. Scorpio eyes particularly express this quality – usually beautiful (and always noticeable) with a piercing intensity that both draws you to them but then forces you to look away.

This is a quiet, remain-in-the-background kind of sign. But it is not a wallflower. It merges into the background as a kind of camouflage and loves to see whilst not being seen – not for Scorpio the showiness of Leo or Libra, nor the brashness of Aries or Sagittarius. Outward display reveals something of the inner man (or woman), and that is alien to Scorpio.

It is by nature secretive and private. What it knows (and it does know plenty), it prefers to keep to itself. Not least of which is the innermost secrets of its own complex personality. Prying into its personal life is to commit the cardinal sin. It will react immediately, causing the perpetrators to see, and probably feel, the famous sting.

Like Taurus, Scorpio tends to react violently when other

people try and force it to do something it does not want to, or to accept ideas that are not its own. Not that either sign is adverse to imposing its will on others, but that's different! The reaction, however, takes an entirely different form. With Taurus, it is blind bestial fury – a great deal of noise, the smashing of inanimate objects and the banging of doors. With Scorpio it takes on a menacingly quiet form. You can physically feel the icy blast from its unblinking gaze. What is worse, you instinctively get the feeling that behind that malevolent gaze is a mind that is planning revenge. Brrrr, just thinking about it gives me the creeps!

But enough about this side of Scorpio. What about the other, less-documented side – its caring nature? This is, after all, a water sign, and like the other two it is emotionally motivated. But the liquid in Scorpio is more like the molten rock of the interior of a volcano than the unfathomable density of Cancer or the ever-flowing waters of Pisces. Still, like the other two, Scorpio cares – how it cares! So much so, that the very intensity of its own emotions can be frightening. Which is why it so often tries to keep the cap on, so to speak. It is as if it is instinctively aware that should it let go and allow the fires of volcanic emotion to vent their force, the result could be uncontrollable. The icy exterior of this quiet introvert is every bit as much a protective shield as is Cancer's crusty shell. Both are attempts to hide a vulnerable centre.

Life for Scorpio is a constant struggle with turbulent emotions in an intensely private world, which only rarely does it allow anyone to share. Which is such a pity, for it has so much to contribute – if only it could learn to harness the power of its own, very personal, lightning charge.

♐ Sagittarius

With Jupiter's vitality, the Archer arms his bow,
'Tis freedom's gift to speak his mind
Be it friend or be it foe.

There is the sweet, clear air of truth, honesty and openness about Sagittarius. Probably what makes it so refreshing is because it follows the intense extremes of Scorpio.

Sagittarius is the polarity of Gemini and the two have a lot in common. Both are restless and changeable; both are adaptable and versatile. There is, however, more depth in Sagittarius. The difference stems from the fire element, for both signs are mutable and positive. The warmth and energizing force of fire gives body to the rather cold and somewhat frivolous intellectuality of Gemini. The result is similar but more reassuring.

Whereas Gemini seeks surface knowledge, spread thinly over as wide a field as it can manage, Sagittarius requires depth. The ability to study and the need for information is the same, but the results are often much more substantial, and for the greater good of all. However, this stronger side of the Sagittarian character may take some time to surface. The immaturity of youth may well have to slip by before these mature characteristics are allowed to interfere with its sheer enjoyment of life. They can lie dormant for the greater part of its life, but they will eventually be recognized and used by the archer.

Sagittarius, above all else, requires freedom of movement and expression. Independence is a right it assumes from the outset. Never try to cage it, for unlike Gemini, who will wilt and fade in captivity, Sagittarius will simply break free and the chances are you will never see it again!

This independent spirit is the essence of Sagittarius. It is a strange quirk, though, that although it tends to dislike discipline and authority – it really does respect them and needs their steadying hand. By the same rule of thumb, for all it likes to be seen as an independent thinker, it tends to stick with the old order of things. Its religious and political leanings (and it is drawn to both) are usually traditional.

It is as if it needs an anchor to hold on to, whilst enjoying its apparent independence. As a teenager it may well be the first to leave home – to try life on its own terms – but it will reserve the right to return to the safety of familiar surroundings, whenever the urge takes it.

The open honesty of the Sagittarian make-up is both refreshing and exceedingly irksome. It says what it thinks, using plan unadulterated language and never stops to think that it may be hurting the feelings of more sensitive folk. The truth, it argues, never hurt anyone. Perhaps not, but a little bit of tact and diplomacy can help soften the blow! This, however, is never found in Sagittarius. It is a clumsy, blundering sign which will walk all over your feet and your feelings! If you bruise easily, on either count, steer clear. Don't say I didn't warn you!

Life for Sagittarius is an exciting gamble, with the odds well stacked in its favour. It arms itself with honest, warm vitality, and an independent spirit, as it plays the game of life to the full.

♑ Capricorn

Upon Life's mountain ranges the sons of Saturn seek,
Ambition drives their measured tread
To reach the highest peak.

This negative sign is the last earth element and cardinal quality. Capricorn begins as the sun reaches the Tropic of Capricorn and is as far away from us, in the Northern Hemisphere, as it can be. This is therefore a cold austere sign.

Practical and cautious, the goat thrives on work and ambition. Even as a child its outlook is serious. The world is a difficult place, full of obstacles and challenges that have to be overcome before anything can be achieved, and Capricorn's need is to succeed. Sights are set high; plans and provisions laid for the long, hard struggle ahead. Then slowly, with great tenacity, perseverance and patience, it begins to move forward.

To know if it is likely to reach the pinnacle of achievement, try looking around at all the successful men and women you know, particularly those in the business world. The chances are that more than a small proportion of them will be Capricorn sun signs. You can take my word for it that the rest – were you to see their birth charts – are likely to have the sign strong in them somewhere.

The combination of earth (practicality and materialism) with cardinal (enterprise, initiative, push) is indeed a very successful one, at least in materialistic terms. On an emotional level this sign leaves a lot to be desired. Emotions can interfere with ambitions. Home ties can hold it back. It is very aware of the pitfalls of allowing emotions to get the upper hand. This is the least likely sign to let its heart rule its head. However, once it does commit itself to a relationship, it does so for life. Responsibilities, even emotional ones, are taken very seriously.

If I appear to be making this sign seem a bit of a wet blanket, I'm sorry, but in a lot of ways it is. It does, however, have one saving grace, and a rather surprising one – a delightful sense of humour. When it laughs its rather grim exterior transforms and, just briefly, you can see the inner person. The laugh itself is often loud and raucous.

When Capricorn predominates a chart – and particularly when it contains the Moon (further information in the next chapter) – life can become a very dreary affair: all work and no play; little or no light refreshment of either a physical or a mental kind. Relaxation does not come easy to Capricorn. When it is not working, it is worrying. This can make life very difficult for the poor individuals who have to live in close proximity.

On top of this – dare I say it – it does have the tendency to become miserly over finances. Money matters are of utmost importance to it. Debts have to be paid, bills have to be met. Money in the bank is a vital necessity, a security to safeguard the future. These heavy qualities will be mitigated if Capricorn is mixed with air or fire signs. If the association is with water, things are likely to be even more dour.

Life is a serious business for Capricorn. It is a slow uphill struggle to reach the top of its own particular mountain. I wonder if, when it gets there, it finally realizes that a summit can be a very cold and lonely place?

♒ Aquarius

Children of Uranus uniquely see alone
Through the far side of a rainbow,
Tomorrows they have known.

Aquarius is the last of the positive air signs. It is also the last in the fixed group, an anomaly in itself. How can air be fixed? It's never static. Maybe this irreconcilable combination gives Aquarius its reputation for eccentricity and instability.

It is, indeed, a strange mixture. Air needs to be free and personal freedom is important to the Waterbearer. On a personal level it is strongly reminiscent of Sagittarius, but without the carefree attitude. The fixed quality seems to hold Aquarius back, confining the would-be free-spirit within restrictive confines. The result is a rebellious personality, resenting authority and always wanting to change the status quo.

Aquarius needs to be different. It feels different, it is different! Its polarity, Leo, wants to be noticed – and so does Aquarius and it doesn't much care whether it is with approval or not. In fact, it often seems to have a perverse desire to shock.

At the present time, as the new Age of Aquarius rises over the horizon, this sign must be feeling its significance more than most. Changes are on the way for all of us – whether we want them or not – and the changes are likely to be Aquarian in make-up.

Aquarius is humanitarian in its outlook, caring for the good of the whole, rather than the individual. In fact, it will willingly sacrifice the individual for the sake of the many. Which is fine, unless *you* happen to be the individual.

The first tentative influence of the Age of Aquarius was felt in the Sixties, whilst the Age of Pisces was still very much with us. The hippy movement of flower power, and a 'make love, not war' philosophy, came into its own during this decade. This movement identifies strongly with both signs. The 'Let's be different; Let's rebel against the old order of things' is purely Aquarian. The preoccupation with flowers, and mind-bending drugs (which make reality less real and thereby more acceptable) is totally Piscean. As the decades have passed, the Piscean influence has become less and less noticeable, but the humanitarian ideals remain – *Aquarius dawns!*

Within this rather peculiar sign are found the inventors of our world, the forward-looking scientists. It is the sign of genius – often eccentric genius, but true genius nevertheless. Paradoxically, a large percentage of those troubled with mental illness also falls within this group. It is a fine line – or so they say – between genius and insanity and Aquarius is destined to walk this tightrope.

Another peculiarity of Aquarius is that although it is futuristic in outlook, seeing tomorrow long before the rest of us, it can often get itself stuck in yesterday. It may be the innovator of new ideas – in the fashion sense, for instance – but it tends to stick with them long after others have moved on. The Oldest Teenager in town, still wearing his 1960s' gear, is probably an Aquarian! Is this the strange result of the combination of fixed quality with air element?

Emotionally, Aquarius finds it hard to equate on a one-to-one basis, preferring friendship to deep, passionate relationships. It gives off an air of coldness and yet is deeply compassionate and humanitarian. It immerses itself in causes such as the Green Movement, Animal Rights, Save the Rain-Forests, and Feed the World.

Life for Aquarius is a revolution against the old order for the benefit of future generations. It lives in tomorrow today and cares little for the ideals of yesterday. It may be eccentric and somewhat unstable but it truly cares for humanity, and doesn't humanity need all the care it can get?

♒ Pisces

Ah, sweet and gentle dreamer,
Such artistry contrives, with Neptune's trap,
So tender set, to dream away your lives.

Pisces is the last sign of all. It is negative, water and mutable: a restless, emotional mixture. Intuition is its forte and Piscean intuition can be uncanny. All the knowledge of the other 11 signs has been passed on to Pisces and somehow it finds this overwhelming. All that knowledge and responsibility is just too much – so the need for Pisces is to escape reality, to turn its back on what is, in favour of what might or could be.

In this sign the distinction between dreams and reality often merge and frequently tends towards some form of escapism; not necessarily of the alcoholic or drugs kind, although Pisces should always be aware of the dangers of both where it is concerned. A more positive form of Piscean escapism is the lure of the entertainment world, where dreams can at least appear to become real.

Another form of escapism which appeals is life in religious communities – often those of closed orders – where the security of devotion and denial, within cloistered walls, shuts out the harshness of the world outside. Pisces can also escape into one or other of the art forms – music particularly appeals. Many poets, painters and composers are born with Sun or Moon or some other prominent feature of their birth chart in this last sign of the zodiac.

If only Pisces would face up to the world, see things as they really are – it is so well equipped to cope! Its mutable quality gives it adaptability and versatility. The strong emotional content of its water element senses when things are wrong and intuitively knows what is required to put them right. The gifts it possesses could help to put the world to rights, if only it could find the will to use them.

A very noticeable thing about this sign is that, from time to time, it seems to want to get away from people, even within the family circle. It has a need for isolation – to be left completely alone, and there is a reason for this.

Pisces is supersensitive – not in a touchy Cancerian way – but in its ability to tune-in to the emotions of other people. Sometimes these external vibrations arrive in such quantities that they result in inner confusion and a kind of loss of identity. Time by itself is necessary to allow Pisces' own inner self to resurface. If this time alone is interfered with, the result can be complete breakdown and a total loss of reality. Like the Scorpio secrecy, or the Cancerian hard exterior, this periodic need for solitude is a protective necessity.

Pisces, like the other restless mutable sign, Gemini, works better when it is mixed with a practical earth sign. Fire too can be a useful additive, providing the necessary spark to make dreams come true. If, however, Pisces is mixed with other water signs, its super-sensitive over-emotional nature is exaggerated and the result is an imbalance which is difficult to handle.

Life for Pisces is seen through rose-coloured spectacles. It is gentle and caring but far too emotionally sensitive for its own good. Its answer is often to escape into an unreal world of its own making.

Summary of the Signs

This, then, is how the signs break down into their various categories and how the different blends give each their own unique character. The influence of the qualities seems to be to present a different view of the elements.

For example: fire in cardinal Aries burns with the uncontrollable red-hot heat of a blazing inferno; in fixed Leo it is expressed as the warmth of summer sun (too much can still burn!); and in mutable Sagittarius the bright flame of enlightenment kindles a burning desire for truth and freedom. Therefore, although each sign is obviously of the fire group, it is the qualities that present us with a differing perspective. Similar subtle distinctions occur in each of the other elements.

In the next chapter we will look at the planets themselves and see how their functions are expressed differently according to the sign in which they are placed. It will be seen how each sign is ruled by a particular planet – a closer look at which will, I hope, help us to a better understanding of both planets and signs.

Chapter 3

The Planets:
Dispersal and Rulerships

To reiterate what I have said before, the sign in which the Sun is found on the date of birth is not the only factor in a birth chart – far from it! In this chapter, I want to examine, not only the Sun but the other nine planets and their dispersal through the various signs of the zodiac. I must state that I am aware that the Sun is not a planet, nor for that matter is the Moon, but for the purpose of interpretation in astrology they are expressed as such. Accepting the above definition, there are ten planets to examine. They are: the Sun, Moon, Mercury, Venus, Mars, Jupiter, Saturn, Uranus, Nepture and Pluto. Let us look at them individually, starting with the Moon, our nearest neighbour and in my opinion, one of the most important factors in a birth chart. It has certainly proved of significance when applied to the hereditary patterns to be examined later.

The Moon

The Moon moves through the zodiac faster than any of the other bodies and covers all the signs of the zodiac in the space of one month. Therefore, it is obviously a more personal placing than the Sun, which stays in each sign for between 28 and 30 days.

The sign in which the Moon falls on the date of birth indicates to an astrologer the instinctive behaviour of a person: their mood changes; the highs and lows of their personality. Let us think about that a little more deeply. The most obvious way of explaining is to look at what the pull of the Moon does to the vast oceans of the world. The Moon causes the ebb and flow of the tides (so reminiscent of the emotional mood changes of the sign of Cancer). Naturally enough, the Moon is said to rule this sign.

Rulership needs some explanation, for it is a very important part, not only of chart analysis, but also of hereditary connections. It is as well to understand rulerships thoroughly, before attempting to penetrate some of the complexities to come. Please don't be put off. I will try to explain simply in stages and I think you will find the results well worth the effort. For the moment, let us just accept that the Moon is the ruler of Cancer, and leave it at that.

The Moon is indicative of the emotional make-up of a person. According to the sign in which it is placed, it manifests as instinctive responses. A point to remember: *It is the planets which are the backbone of an astrological analysis. The signs are simply the means by which they express their principles.* What I mean is that no matter where the Moon is found, it will always behave as the Moon. It will not act like the Sun, or Mars: it will always be itself, but the manner of its expression will vary from sign to sign. This is the same for all the planets.

To explain further, let us take a brief look at the Moon in a few of the signs.

Moon in Aries

Aries, as you will remember, is a cardinal, fire sign. When the Moon is found there, the 'me-first' tendencies become instinctive and very noticeable. The temper – never very stable – becomes somewhat erratic. The fluctuating temperament of the planet manifests itself as an irritable and irascible temperament.

Moon in Virgo

The Moon in Virgo, a mutable, earth sign, results in an individual who worries incessantly. The emotional nature of the planet gets bogged down by the sign's natural attention to detail. A person with this position will worry about anything and everything.

Moon in Aquarius

The fixed, air mixture of Aquarius combined with the fluctuation of the Moon leads to erratic behaviour patterns and a very unpredictable nature. The nurturing nature of the planet has difficulty with the detached attitudes of the sign. Tension is an obvious result.

Moon in Cancer

The Moon, as the ruler of Cancer, is naturally at home here. All Cancerian traits are emphasized. The strong family instinct of both sign and planet are in accord with each other. It goes without saying that this placing produces a high emotional level in an individual.

The above descriptions of the Moon indicate that the planet is the driving force and the signs the means by which the individual interprets its specific function.

The Sun

The descriptions given in the previous chapter will serve as typical of the sun signs. However, it is a good point to remember that the Sun does not manifest itself half as strongly as is often stated. It seems to require the backing of at least Mercury, and often one or two more planets, to give full vent to its sign interpretation.

There are a few exceptions. Sun in Aries is often quite recognizable; Sun in Taurus is particularly indicative of the sign's characteristics; and Sun in Leo is always identifiable. This is because the Sun is the ruler of Leo and, like the Moon in Cancer, is at one with its own natural function. The natural function of the Sun is to shine, to be noticed, to radiate the heat of its own being – all totally Leonian.

Mercury

Mercury is a fast-moving planet. It is never seen further than 28° away from the Sun. You might think that this closeness would swamp or burn out its personal function. The opposite is often the case. Mercury seems to reinforce the sign position of the Sun when they are found together. The only instance when the Sun seems to override Mercury is when they are found very (and I do mean *very*) close together. Then Mercury does not operate at its best.

The function of Mercury in a birth chart is to indicate the mentality of a person. It does not show how clever a person is, but rather in what manner their mind works. To clarify the role of Mercury, let us look at this planet in a few signs.

Mercury is said to be the ruler of both Gemini and Virgo.

Mercury in Cancer

As you might imagine, when Mercury falls in Cancer, the emotions tend to colour the thinking. The mind works subconsciously, particularly when it comes to taking in information. The person with this placing often finds that they have knowledge of subjects that they have not actually studied. It seems to stem from an unconscious emotional stimulus activating the memory to store up information, of its own accord. An excellent memory is always indicated by this placing, stemming perhaps from the fact that memory is the central core of the mind, and the fact that Cancer is forever concerned with the past.

Mercury in Libra

Libra is a highly logical sign, so you would think that Mercury would work well when found here. However, although it does seem to indicate good reasoning power, it also endows the person with the ability to see all sides to all questions. This leads to a difficulty in making decisions. The decisions that are finally reached (hopefully they are not required urgently) are almost certain to be the right ones, but they can take forever to get there.

Mercury in Gemini

Like Sun in Leo and Moon in Cancer, Mercury in Gemini is in the sign of its own rulership and therefore works with ease. The mental agility of this placing is fast, super-fast. There is a desire for knowledge and an inventive and lively turn of mind. Great versatility is indicated, but, as always with Gemini, this can cause the person to be too easily satisfied with superficial knowledge. Often this placing is indicative of the jack of all trades (and master of none) type of person.

Mercury in Virgo

Mercury, like Venus, is assigned two rulerships. Not only does it rule Gemini, but it also rules Virgo. In Virgo the analytical and critical qualities of the sign work in conjunction with quickness of mind. The mentality, as with Mercury in Gemini, is quick and sharp. However, in this sign it is put to better use and this placing results in good research workers, capable of long and painstaking work. This positive trait can become obsessional and Virgo's attention to detail may block the view of the overall picture.

Venus

Venus, like Mercury, is fast moving. It is never found more than two signs away from the Sun. In a chart Venus indicates a person's attitude, need, and attraction – or otherwise – to other people. It is also indicative of the desire for material possessions. Let's see how this works.

Venus rules Taurus and Libra.

Venus in Sagittarius

Venus in this freedom-loving sign often indicates a person who is unwilling to commit him or herself on a long-term basis at least in the early years. It indicates a natural friendliness to fellow creatures – animal as well as human – but the sign's fear of losing independence can be a stumbling block to close relationships. On the material front, there is a nonchalant attitude to money and possessions.

Venus in Pisces

The over-emotional and impressionable nature of the sign gives an unrealistic outlook when Venus is placed here. It makes for a gentle, sweet individual, but one that is rather too gullible for his or her own good. Over-sentimentality combines with genuine feelings and the result can be too much of a good thing. On a practical level, money means nothing to people with this placing and often they are hopeless at handling it. They do have an appreciation of beautiful things, not because of their financial value, but simply because they are pleasing to the eye.

Venus in Taurus

Venus is at home in the sign of its rulership, but the less attractive side of the planet often shows itself when placed here. A strongly materialistic attitude to possessions is nearly always indicated. Another noticeable effect is often a lazy streak which, coupled with a love of good food and wine, can lead to a weight-problem. Romantically, this placing indicates passionate affections and a desire to own the object of them! Materialistically, this placing is excellent and finances are likely to be well organized.

Venus in Libra

When placed in the second sign of its rulership, Venus puts on another face. There is still a love of beautiful things (and beautiful people) but of a more aesthetic nature. The outer appearance is very refined and graceful. A diplomatic manner is often evident and is guaranteed to attract other people. The trouble with this placing is that it often results in a person who is in love with the idea of being in love rather than one who is able to recognize the real thing. This placing indicates a truly romantic person, and it also bestows an inborn need for the finer things of life.

Mars

Mars in a birth chart indicates the way the aggressive nature is expressed. It is also indicative of the sexual nature of the person. Again let us look at a few examples, noting that Mars is the ruler of Aries.

Mars in Taurus

Taurus is an earthy, practical sign and when Mars is found here the aggressive nature of the planet is applied to practical use. The result is a person who is a hard and tenacious worker, particularly in the practical professions. Only rarely will the violent potential of the sign be allowed to break out – but watch out when it does! The financial implications are good with this placing and money may be earned by hard physical labour. Mars in Taurus is indicative of a very sexy nature. The impulsiveness of the planet combined with the sensuousness of the sign indicates very physical relationships. Jealousy can cause big problems.

Mars in Scorpio

The aggressive nature of the planet combines with the deeply emotional nature of the sign with problematic results. The tendency of the sign to repress the emotions means that the aggressiveness of the planet is kept capped and may eventually blow with volcanic force. Like Mars in Taurus, this placement leads to jealousy and possessiveness in relationships. A person with this combination will tend to watch their lover's every move and want to know his or her innermost feelings.

Mars in Aries

The impulsive nature of both planet and sign point to someone who has a powerful urge to take the lead. Together this planet and sign are a great energy force, but a tendency to be accident prone is indicated, due to the impulsive nature of both. Mars feels at home in the red-hot atmosphere of Aries. Aggression is given its head and channelled into positive outlets. Although there may be temper outbursts (dare I say, even tantrums) from time to time, these are merely the safety valves letting off steam! As you might imagine, with both planet and sign in unison, this placing indicates an individual who is strongly sexed.

Jupiter

Jupiter is a much slower-moving planet than any we have looked at so far. It takes about 12 years to pass through all the signs of the zodiac. The function of Jupiter is expansion, whether it be on a physical level or a mental one. Here are a few examples of how Jupiter, which is the ruler of Sagittarius, works in various signs.

Jupiter in Leo

In Leo Jupiter exaggerates the outward showiness of the sign. Leo always loves to shine, but when Jupiter falls within its confines, brightness becomes brilliance! The need to expand can show as extravagance. This placing makes for larger-than-life individuals. Whether they become show-business stars, or settle for the role of teacher (a Jupiterian profession and Leo is always at home with children), or something similar, you cannot fail to notice them.

Jupiter in Capricorn

This placing is a bit difficult to deal with. Jupiter's need is to expand, metaphysically as well as in actuality. Capricorn is the sign of slow and steady progress. How far is not the concern. What matters is the direction, which is always upwards. People who have this combination in their birth charts show a strong sense of responsibility. Restricting the natural expansion of the planet, this sign seems to indicate an individual who lacks cheerfulness and tends to be negative in outlook. A miserly streak is not uncommon.

Jupiter in Sagittarius

In the sign of its rulership Jupiter comes into its own. The outlook is optimistic, generous, jovial and kind. There is a true sense of justice and a great compassion. The intellectual capacity is excellent and has a very good chance of being developed to the full. A love of sport is common as is a love of animals, in particular, horses. However, the tendency to boast, to gamble and to be reckless is also prominent.

Saturn

Saturn's function is the exact opposite of Jupiter's: that of limitation. It is a slow-moving planet and spends long (but varying) periods in each sign. This is the last of the personal planets. Saturn's placing in a birth chart indicates areas of difficulty, of obstacles to be overcome. It is only by over-coming these obstacles that we can learn the lessons of Saturn and this planet is often called the Great Teacher. If the lessons, difficult though they may be, are learned well, the individual will reap great rewards. Let us have a look at how this planet, the ruler of Capricorn, operates in a few signs.

Saturn in Aries

The ambition and self-reliance of Aries are emphasized and given persistence, therefore this placing can lead to solid achievements but depression may become a great problem. The self-centred make-up of the sign combines with the serious nature of the planet and everything is seen as being directed personally at the individual. Thus a very touchy nature is indicated. Aries (like its ruler Mars) works impuls-ively. Saturn, on the other hand, works slowly from pre-conceived, well-thought-out plans. This can give a stop-go feel to the personality.

Saturn in Gemini

Saturn works well in air signs for it seems to give the stability they often lack. In Gemini the placing gives intellectual ability and the mind is steady and can be profound. It may be a cold placing for the personality, however, for Gemini has very little emotional depth and Saturn is an unemotional planet. This combination makes for good teachers or lecturers, but a lack of warmth may inhibit the pupils.

Saturn in Capricorn

In the sign of its rulership, Saturn, as you might expect, produces a serious individual. The result of this combination is practical ability, a sense of discipline, patience, and perseverance. Ambition is paramount. This placing usually produces successful people, but whether they are happy individuals depends on the rest of the chart, as Saturn in its own sign can be almost too heavy to handle.

The Outer Planets: Uranus, Neptune and Pluto

These three planets spend so much time in one single sign that they tend to be less personal in their interpretation. They appear to be indicative of a specific generation, but there are exceptions, of course. They are of personal importance to a person when they are found to be the Sun or Moon ruler, or of even greater significance, the ruler of the Ascendant. We will look at rulerships next and the following chapter deals with the personal points – the most important of which is the Ascendant.

The rulerships of the outer planets are: Uranus rules Aquarius; Neptune rules Pisces; Pluto rules Scorpio.

Rulerships and how they are applied to the Birth Chart

Rulerships are a very important part of the analysis of a birth chart, so it is necessary for us to take a closer look at them.

The rulerships are:

Aries	is ruled by	Mars
Taurus	is ruled by	Venus
Gemini	is ruled by	Mercury
Cancer	is ruled by	Moon

Leo	is ruled by	Sun
Virgo	is ruled by	Mercury
Libra	is ruled by	Venus
Scorpio	is ruled by	Pluto
Sagittarius	is ruled by	Jupiter
Capricorn	is ruled by	Saturn
Aquarius	is ruled by	Uranus
Pisces	is ruled by	Neptune

We saw in our look at the dispersal of the planets how most of them work well in the signs of their rulership. But there is more to it than that. It is important to memorize which planet rules which sign. When an astrologer begins to analyse a chart he or she first sorts out which planet is placed where. Then the positions of the rulers of the planets are checked because it is a blending of the two that makes up the individual. For example, suppose it was found that the Sun was placed in Scorpio and the Moon in Sagittarius, with Pluto the ruler of Scorpio being found in Leo and Jupiter also being located in Leo. How would you begin to analyse these findings?

My own personal method (which is a first-glance short-cut to the final analysis) would be to write down the sign for the Sun next to the sign for the Moon, draw a line underneath them and put the sign for the Sun Ruler and the sign for the Moon Ruler side by side underneath them, thus:

Scorpio with Sagittarius
Leo with Leo

which sums up as, First Leo; Second Scorpio; Third Sagittarius.

The above would tell me that the basic character of the subject in question would be a blend of the above signs, with the Leo content probably showing the strongest, but with the emotional and secretive nature of Scorpio indicating a very possessive and jealous character. The Sagittarian influence would add to the warmth of the Leo but cause an inner conflict because of the instinctive (Moon) need for freedom (Sagittarius) vying with the emotional possessiveness of Scorpio.

This is only a quick, overall blend of the characteristics, but when the full analysis is worked out, the results usually concur.

I would then do the same kind of 'sum' with Mercury (this

time looking to analyse the mentality of the subject). Let's say that the subject had Mercury in Libra and Venus in Capricorn. It would, therefore, be a blend of these two signs that made up the basic mentality. I would interpret it as, a logical outlook, combined with a sense of justice and fair play (Libra), together with a practical application of the mind to learning and to applying the knowledge to achieve ambitions (Capricorn).

There are various blendings of planets and rulers depending on what part of the analysis you are looking at. But the rule remains the same; the planets together with the placing of their rulers are blended together. When more than one planet is involved, the sign containing the highest number of planets seems to assume priority.

I'll give you two further examples. Both myself and my husband are Taurus sun signs and we both have Venus (the ruler of Taurus) in Aries, but I have Moon in Gemini with Mercury also in this sign, and he has Moon in Capricorn with Saturn in Aries. The blends, therefore, go like this. I come out as Gemini with Taurus and Aries and he comes out as Aries with Taurus and Capricorn. Two very different results although both sun signs and both Sun Rulers are the same.

Finally, in respect of rulership there are two other points of significance in chart analysis to be kept in mind. They are a Final Dispositor and the case of Mutual Reception. Both sound complicated, but are quite easy to understand.

First the Final Dispositor, which is a very important factor when it occurs. As we have seen above, each sign has a planet as its ruler. When one single planet is found in the sign of its own rulership, then that planet becomes the ruler, so to speak, of the whole chart. The *only* time you can have a Final Dispositor is when *one single* planet is found in the sign of its own rulership, e.g. Pluto in Scorpio while none of the other planets are in the signs of their own rulership.

Mutual Reception simply means that one planet is found in the sign of another's rulership when that same planet is in the sign of its ruler. For instance Mercury in Libra and Venus in Virgo. Libra is ruled by Venus; Venus is in Virgo which is ruled by Mercury. When this occurs the two planets seem to help each other out and work well and strongly together.

Chapter 4

Personal Points and Houses (or Overlays)

The personal points are an essential part of a person's birth chart. As their name suggests, they are personal to each, being arrived at by the calculation of the exact moment of birth at the exact place of birth (or as near as is possible). The more accurate the birth data the more accurate the analysis, not only of the personal points themselves but also of the whole chart. This is because it is from the Ascendant (or rising sign) that the pattern of the rest of the chart evolves.

The positioning of signs and planets within the birth chart are dependent upon the point of the Ascendant. Thus it personalizes each and every chart and produces a map (or blueprint) of the heavens, as seen from a specific point on earth (the birth place), at a specific moment in time (the birth time). This blueprint is unique, being as individual as each and every human being. Thus, you can see the importance of the personal points in a birth-chart analysis. Now let's look at them in more detail.

The Ascendant/Descendent Axis

The Ascendant is the specific degree of the sign that is rising in the east at the moment of birth. The Descendent is the opposite degree (its polarity) which is setting in the west at the same moment in time. This is a point to remember: the Ascendant and Descendent go together; you cannot have one without the other. Much more stress is put on the Ascendant because it is the most recognizable feature of a birth chart. The Descendent tends to be neglected. This is a pity, for there is no doubt that the interpretations of the different signs on the Ascendant are coloured by the effect of their polarities, and

thus they should not be interpreted as simply another sun sign.
If they are, the results are unsatisfactory.

Let us take a brief look at the signs when they are on the
Ascendant.

Ascendant: Aries

The typical sun-sign interpretation of a self-orientated individual
is even more personalized in this position. But the double
cardinal quality of the combined Ascendant/Descendent (Aries/
Libra) gives it more impetus. People with this sign rising
intend to get somewhere in life and intend doing it their own
way. The mixture of fire and air elements can work in one of
two ways (naturally, with Libra's need for balance).

1 Air can fan fire's flames and cause them to burn with such ferocity
that they consume the air and consequently die out themselves. This
is the shooting-star type of individual – offering such potential, but
fizzling into nothing after a beautiful but brief moment of glory.

2 Fire can heat air, warming it, and giving the necessary spark to its
intellectual capacity. In this type of personality, the two work well
together. Air keeps fire alive, and fire adds warmth to chilly
unemotional air. This type of Aries individual is less self-centred and
more people-orientated. They are still achievers and go-getters, but
not at the expense of other people.

Ascendant: Taurus

There is much depth in this Ascendant. The solid (and stolid)
strength of Taurus is coloured by the magnetic intensity of
Scorpio and, whether for better or worse, this is a powerful
combination. The fixed nature of both signs adds to the
inflexibility, making a totally (and I do mean *totally*) immovable force. It would take a nuclear explosion to shift them, and
even then they could possibly withstand it.

The water element of Scorpio when added to the earth of
Taurus makes for very heavy going. Water plus earth in this
case equals *mud*. This muddiness adds to the immovability.
The solid practicality of the earth element is infiltrated by

water's emotional content and can result in a rather difficult personality.

At first glance, this Ascendant personality may appear to be easy to deal with, but remember that it is chameleon Scorpio which is also involved. Tread carefully, pick your steps with caution, or you will get swallowed up in a quagmire of emotional inflexibility and excessive possessiveness.

Ascendant: Gemini

Gemini as an Ascendant sign has more depth and less superficiality than as a sun sign. The bright flame of Sagittarius gives it much more sparkle and warmth.

However, the double mutable quality does increase the restlessness of the nature. This Ascendant needs to be able to move. Both literally and intellectually, it can't do with being tied down. The air/fire mix of this Ascendant can be a very good combination and there appears to be less chance of the fire burning itself out (as in the fire/air Aries combination) so long as freedom of movement is maintained.

The intellectual qualities of Gemini expand and seek greater knowledge in this position. However, busybody tendencies are exacerbated. Don't ever tell your secrets to someone with this Ascendant – they just can't keep them! To think something is to say it, is a philosophy inborn in both signs. The brutal honesty of Sagittarius when added to the limitless vocabulary of Gemini makes for a *very sharp-tongued* individual.

Ascendant: Cancer

A Cancerian Ascendant, like the sun sign, is prone to fluctuating moods, but the practical, cautious nature of Capricorn gives a heavier feel to the personality. The double cardinal quality indicates that this Ascendant has somewhere to go and something to achieve. The water/earth combination can get bogged down but is less likely to do so than the earth/water combination of the Taurus Ascendant. The waters of Cancer still manage to flow, albeit slowly, over the solid earth of Capricorn.

One outcome of this combination can be that of the domineering parent. Cancer always indicates a tendency to want to hold on to the offspring, but when it is on the Ascendant, then the emotional content of water, combines with the practicality of earth to produce a parental overkill. The domineering Victorian father figure is typical of this type of Cancerian personality. The welfare of the offspring is the only motivation, but that does not stop the result becoming intolerable to those subjected to its rigorism.

Ascendant: Leo

This Ascendant, as you might expect, needs to be noticed. Both Leo and its polarity, Aquarius, are not signs you can ignore. The icy detached attitude of Aquarius cools down some of the Leo warmth, but does not take away the need to shine. Again, in this combination we find a blend of fire and air. Once more, on the whole, it works well except that Leo as an Ascendant may not handle close one-to-one relationships as well as it does as a sun sign.

The double fixed quality (as with the Taurus Ascendant) makes for a very immovable character. Sometimes this rigidity can be mistaken for an indication of Taurus in a subject, but there is far more panache and slightly less rigidity when Leo rises.

Ascendant: Virgo

The Pisces influence gives a gentler feel to Ascendant Virgo than you find with the sun sign. A greater emotional expression shows through the personality. The critical side of Virgo is less harsh – not missing – just softer in make-up. The analytical approach also loses some of its sharpness and at times can even take on the fuzziness of Pisces thinking.

What is very often indicated by this combination is an interest in the medical profession. Both signs have a need to serve and Virgo's capacity for seeing things in clear-cut terms overrules the Piscean need to escape reality. The result is very often a truly caring (water) and practically helpful (earth) individual.

The Ascendant signs, Libra to Pisces, simply reverse the above descriptions. For example, take Libra rising. The same blending occurs as with Aries/Libra except that the Libra tendencies are more externalized and noticeable and the Aries ones more muted and less forceful. Air seems to take precedence over fire (as with Gemini/Sagittarius) in this case.

The Midheaven Axis (The MC/IC)

The Midheaven (MC) is the degree of the sign which is culminating – or directly overhead – at the moment of birth. The MC is an underestimated personal point, being relegated, more often than not, simply to that area of a person's chart connected with the career and the aims in life. Whilst this interpretation to some extent is correct, it is not the only function of the Midheaven. Its opposite point, the Nadir (or IC) is often ignored altogether. (MC and IC are abbreviations for Medium Coeli and Immum Coeli, being the Latin for Midheaven and Deepest Heaven, the Nadir.)

These two points work in conjunction with each other, much like the Ascendant/Descendent, but often with more co-operation between them. I have found that the Midheaven acts in a similar way to the Ascendant, but that it is seen in the basic characteristics of a person rather than in the outer personality.

The IC is less noticeable but seems to be more the sub-conscious motivation for the expression of the sign on the Midheaven, which is in itself quite logical, since the Nadir is the natural position of the sign of Cancer and of its ruler, the Moon.

One of my discoveries from research into hereditary patterns is that a strong connection appears to exist between the Sun and the Midheaven and the Moon and the Ascendant. I interpret this in the following way: the Sun indicates the conscious characteristics of an individual and the Moon shows the emotional instincts; in the same way the Ascendant indicates the outer (instinctive) personality and the Midheaven the conscious motivations and ideals.

Bearing this in mind, analysis of the Midheaven assumes a greater importance than simply being an indicator of career potential. The blending of the signs involved is similar to the above interpretations of the Ascendant signs, but remember that what is being looked at is the conscious rather than the instinctive side of the personality.

What of the rulers of the personal points? The ruler of the sign on the Ascendant is said to be the ruler of the whole chart (unless a Final Dispositor exists, as explained previously). It is, therefore, a very important planet. The ruler of the Midheaven is also important and should not be forgotten.

My own way of dealing with the blendings involved is to approach the matter in the same way as I do the characteristic, mentality signs, etc. In other words, I write down the Ascendant sign next to the one for the Midheaven and then as before, place the signs of their rulerships side by side beneath them. For example, say a person had Ascendant Aquarius and Midheaven Sagittarius, with Uranus in Gemini and Jupiter also in Gemini, the results would be:

First – Gemini; Second – Aquarius; Third – Sagittarius.

However, if Uranus was in Taurus and Jupiter in Gemini the results would be:

First – Aquarius; Second – Sagittarius; Third – Taurus and Fourth – Gemini.

Get the idea? This should not be taken as a final analysis of the personality, for it is a first-glance summing up which indicates the likely results of a closer examination.

Houses or Overlays

Let me say at the outset that I do not lay a great deal of importance on the traditional meaning and interpretation of house signs. I have never been completely satisfied with the results of using them, and have often found them confusing in chart analysis. Nevertheless, an introduction to them is needed before we start to investigate the hereditary patterns. They feature significantly (though not in the traditional or established sense) in my findings.

What, then, are houses – or, as I prefer to call them, overlays?

Houses are said to refer to the areas of everyday life-on-earth. I have always found the jump from signs to houses, with the sign function being interpreted as areas of life, rather contrived and unsatisfactory. For example, since Taurus is a very possessive and acquisitive sign it thereby indicates that the house of Taurus (the second house) should be concerned with possessions. Personally, I have never found this jump from characteristic interpretation to synonymous areas of life altogether convincing. But, as with all things concerning this vast subject, if it works for you, then by all means use it.

Most house systems (and there are at least 20) take the degree of the Ascendant sign as their starting point, being the beginning, or the cusp, of the first house (the house of Aries). By various methods, the rest of the houses follow the natural order of the zodiac. Therefore, if a person has Sagittarius on the Ascendant, this sign is said to be on the cusp of the first house. In other words, an overlay of signs, beginning with Sagittarius and following in natural order, is superimposed on the chart. Taking the above example, if say the sun was found in the sign of Gemini, it is likely (dependent on which system is used) that the Sun would be found to be in the seventh house (the house of Libra).

The traditional meanings of the houses are:

First House House of Aries	Physical appearance, temperament everything pertaining to the self.
Second House House of Taurus	Possessions of all kinds. Money, worldly resources.
Third House House of Gemini	Family, particularly siblings. Education, speech, transport, short journeys.
Fourth House House of Cancer	The home, the parents or, more particularly, the mother.
Fifth House House of Leo	Children, creativity, pleasures, speculation, sport.
Sixth House House of Virgo	Work and subordinates, health.
Seventh House House of Libra	Relationships and partnerships.

Eighth House	Legacies, insurance, sex, birth and death and
House of Scorpio	attitudes towards same.
Ninth House	Further education, research, long-distance
House of Sagittarius	travel, languages, political and religious
	beliefs.
Tenth House	The career, ambitions and social status.
House of Capricorn	Responsibilities generally.
Eleventh House	Friends and acquaintances, group activities,
House of Aquarius	clubs, societies etc.
Twelfth House	Service to others, self-sacrifice, escapism in all
House of Pisces	forms.

I would like, at this point, to suggest an alternative interpretation of the overlay pattern in birth-chart analysis. This has arisen from my hereditary findings. Incidentally, the hereditary connection only works when using the equal house system. Other systems produce similar but random and inconsistent results. Therefore, it seems that perhaps this system is to be preferred, but not necessarily for use with the traditional interpretation of houses.

What I would suggest, at least on an investigatory trial basis, is that the houses be interpreted as shadow signs. Now, I know that this goes against all traditional teachings. Nevertheless, I have tried it out myself on a good number of charts *and it works!*

I am not suggesting that the house signs be interpreted in exactly the same way as planets in signs, but rather as an additional colouring. To use a totally Taurean metaphor, the planets are the basic ingredients; the signs the way the recipe is blended together to make up the dish; and the overlay (or houses) are the condiments that are added by the individual, to their own taste, to give the meal its final flavour.

This is how it works.

I, myself, have a stellium (a large interconnecting groupage of planets) starting with the Sun in the last degrees of Taurus, then Saturn and Uranus (I place these two planets together because they are only minutes of a degree apart in my case) at 00° Gemini (Uranus is my Chart Ruler), then the Moon at

02° Gemini, crossing the Geminian IC the stellium ends with Mercury (my Final Dispositor) in conjunction with Jupiter (my MC Ruler). All these planets are less than 30° apart. This, as you might imagine, is a forceful mix and very Geminian in make-up, yet having something of the solidity of Taurus about it. This tight groupage falls in the house of Cancer and Leo. Whilst I am obviously very Geminian in make-up and certainly cannot deny my stubborn Taurean streak, there is within me a Cancerian undercurrent. I certainly display Cancerian touchiness and my world revolves around my home and family. Even my interest in astrology centres around past ties and family connections. On top of which, the dreadful pain and sense of loss I felt when my children left home was truly Cancerian in nature.

As to the Leo – well, I have to admit it, I do enjoy being the centre of attention and yes, I can be a bit of a show-off. I am told tales by my parents of myself as a child and, quite honestly, I must have been an obnoxious, precocious, little know-it-all. Yes Leo is certainly a part of the mix. The shadow blending of the house signs works in my case, and in a great many others. Why not try it for yourselves?

Before moving on to the next chapter, which deals with aspects of the interrelationships of planets and/or points and the theory of harmonics, I would like to introduce the reader to what is known as absolute longitude. This sounds complicated, but isn't.

Absolute longitude is simply the breakdown of the signs of the zodiac into their geometric degrees. The zodiac, like all circles, is made up of 360°. Each sign contains 30° and there are 12 signs, making up the full 360°. The first degree of the zodiac is 00° 00′ of Aries – which in absolute longitude terms is the same, 00° 00′. The first degree of the sign of Taurus is 00° 00′ Taurus, but in absolute longitude it is 30° 00′. Following the same mathematics (and remembering that each sign contains 30°), if the Sun, say, was found at 25° 45′ of Scorpio then the absolute longitude for the Sun would be 235° 45′. That is all there is to it. Every planet or point in a chart has its own absolute longitudinal degree. It is easier to use this when looking for aspects – and very significant when dealing with the degree connections within families.

Absolute longitude also helps to explain one of the things which troubled me for a long time when I first took up astrology – incidentally, with a view to disproving such nonsense! Most people who want to discredit astrology point out with glee that, as the centuries have passed, the actual zodiac (or their constellations) have moved from where they were originally seen from the earth. Thus, if you are born with the Sun in such and such a sign – the Sun in actual fact is no longer likely to be found in that constellation. This fact cannot be argued with and it troubled me even when I found to my surprise that birth-chart analysis did appear to work.

It wasn't until I had advanced much further in my studies of the subject that I found an acceptable explanation. True, the constellations have moved away. But as modern followers of astrology recognize, it is neither the planets themselves, nor the signs, that are actually influencing the individual. The apparent cause (and it is not yet really understood) seems to be the constant bombardment from space of various pulsating waves and the interference of these by the interreactions of the movement of the planets (including the earth) around the centre of our solar system, the Sun. Astrological signs are simply symbolic interpretations.

If, when looking towards the heavens at a given moment in time (the birth time), from a specific point on earth (the place of birth) on a specific day (the birth date), a planet or point is seen at 55° 20' of absolute longitude, this would be interpreted as being 25° 20' of the sign of Taurus – whether or not the actual constellation was in that part of the sky or not. The part of the sky that the ancient astrologers interpreted as 25° 20' of Taurus is still that same part of the sky (in absolute longitude) even though the constellation itself has moved away from this position. Simple, isn't it? When this fact dawned on me, a great many of my recurring doubts about the validity of astrology vanished, never to return.

The next chapter looks at the interreaction of planets on one another which is called the aspects, and the new and interesting theory of harmonics (or wave patterns).

Chapter 5

Aspects and Harmonics

What are aspects? Aspects are the interconnection of the function of two or more planets or points when, viewed from the earth, they appear at certain distances from each other. There are a great many aspects but we shall examine only a few of them for the purpose of this book. Aspects are given names which are symbolic of their geometric features. This will become clear as we progress.

Traditionally the major aspects are:

The Conjunction	0° apart	orb 8°
The Opposition	180° apart	orb 6°
The Square	90° apart	orb 4°
The Trine	120° apart	orb 4°

Aspects of medium strength are:

The Sextile	60° apart	orb 2°
The Quincunx	150° apart	orb 1°

Aspects of minor strength are:

The Semisquare	45° apart	orb 30'
The Semisextile	30° apart	orb 30'

An orb is the distance from exactitude. They are somewhat flexible, according to the aspect and planets involved and in relation to the rest of the chart. It is only with experience that an ability is developed to decide which is the correct orb to use for a particular aspect in a particular chart. For those who are just beginning, the above orbs should prove an adequate guideline. I have found them to be reasonably accurate in analysis. There are several more minor aspects but most are not used in everyday analysis.

Traditionally, some aspects are 'easy' and others 'difficult'. But it should be remembered that the result of dealing successfully with the so-called difficult ones can lead to a satisfactory conclusion, whereas the so-called easy ones may indicate a waste of talent. Nothing in astrology is as simple as it first appears.

In today's astrology the interpretation of easy and difficult aspects is more flexible than of old, and I find that it is the actual connection itself between the bodies or points that is of major importance. Like everything else in birth-chart analysis, aspects must be seen and considered in conjunction with the rest of the information that makes up the complete picture. For that reason I will not bother to separate the above groups of aspects into their easy or difficult categories. If you get to know your planets and your signs, the interpretation of a particular aspect in a particular chart will automatically present itself.

What are harmonics?

I do not pretend to understand exactly what the cause and effect of the harmonics of aspects actually are. However, they seem to go a long way to explaining how aspects actually work. Harmonics are waves. In today's world we are beginning to understand the theory of waves – radio signals for example – or light waves. It seems that the earth is constantly being bombarded by waves of various kinds from outer space. The planets, as they move around the Sun, give every appearance of generating waves of changing density and strength as their orbits interconnect in ever-changing but consistent patterns. The earth itself, remember, is giving out waves as well as receiving them and is itself moving and inter-reacting with the other planets as they all orbit their central star, the Sun.

Harmonics are quite easy to understand. Since, in astrology, we are always dealing with a circle (the 360 absolute longitudinal degrees of the zodiac), the number of the harmonic is the number of times the aspect degree divides into the circle. Take, for instance, the square aspect – which is the fourth harmonic. The 90° angle of the square aspect divides evenly four times into the 360° of the zodiac. Therefore, the length of the fourth harmonic (or square aspect) is 90°. It is as simple as that!

There is, of course, a great deal more to it: the amplitude of the wave (its power); the phase (the point at which its peak occurs) and, of course, the orb allowable for interpretation purposes (its intensity and where it fades out). All of these issues are certainly worthy of note, but are far too involved for the purpose of this book. Anyone interested in finding out more about harmonics should study several good works on the subject which are available at the present time.

Incidentally, the same is true for the question of Midpoints. I personally find them very informative when it comes to chart interpretation, but inclusion would only serve to complicate this particular book.

The Meaning of Aspects and Harmonic Numbers

The Conjunction or First Harmonic (1H)

The conjunction is the joining together of the bodies or points. The 1H is very significant, being the fundamental harmonic. More often than not, a conjunction indicates the difficulty of making two (or more) diverse planets work well together within one individual. However, when this is achieved – and it often is – the results are well worthwhile.

Judgement of the 1H depends on the nature of the bodies involved, the sign or signs occupied and on the orb. (An orb is the distance from exactitude.)

Let us look at some examples which should not be taken as finite, but are to be seen as only one of many possible ways of interpreting the joining together of the particular bodies, dependent upon the rest of the chart in question.

Sun/Moon 1H
A focal point and an extremely powerful aspect. This may

cause the person to be rather one-sided and have an inability to see the other person's point of view. It can also indicate a certain lack of adaptability. The sign (or signs) that this aspect falls in needs careful examination. (The same is true for the 'shadow sign' of the house or houses.)

Moon/Saturn 1H
This aspect often indicates the ability to work hard and generally gives a strong sense of duty. The subject may lack a sense of fun.

Mercury/Mars 1H
This indicates a lively mind and gives an excess of mental energy. Success often comes with this aspect, as the intellectual capacity of Mercury is given added vigour and push by the Mars influence. However, the nerves can suffer because of a tendency to go beyond one's limitations.

The Opposition or Second Harmonic (2H)

The opposition, as its name implies, indicates strain: two (or more) opposing forces pulling against each other. But, remember that one could not exist without the other and that opposites (or polarities) can also gain much from one another. Therefore, oppositions, although indicating strain, can also give necessary balance. Here are a few examples.

Venus/Mars 2H
The desire nature is very strong. Lively and outgoing but aggressive and uncompromising is the likely combination. Relationships are likely to be difficult due to an argumentative streak combined with an extremely sensitive nature. This opposition can make a person very difficult for other people to understand.

Mercury/Saturn 2H
This aspect often indicates someone who is very strongly self-opinionated. The intellectual ability is considerable but the mentality, like everything else, is overdefensive. Depression can be a problem with this combination.

Jupiter/Uranus 2H
This often indicates a high degree of enthusiasm. Intuition combines with depth of knowledge to enhance the intellectual development. However, lack of moderation and erratic behaviour can slow progress.

The Trine or Third Harmonic (3H)

Trines are the division of the circle by three, making for a connecting distance of 120° (as with the element groupage). Traditionally, trines were said to be 'easy' aspects, but, as stated before, too much of a good thing can lead to poor results. This is particularly so with trines. The bodies in question do seem to be able to co-operate with each other, but the outcome is often very negative – because no effort is required, none is given and therefore nothing is achieved. However, please remember it is the planets involved rather than the aspect which is important. Here are a few examples.

Sun/Mars 3H
The Sun and Mars work well together, no matter what the aspect, and with the trine the outcome is often a person with leadership qualities and great self-confidence. Great courage and powers of endurance are indicated. There is an abundance of energy flow with this combination, but it is often channelled into a play-hard rather than a work-hard outlet.

Moon/Venus 3H
This often indicates a gentle disposition and attractive personality. There is ability at handling other people without them realizing that they are being 'handled'. Popularity is an obvious outcome, but there is also a tendency to rest on one's laurels and to sit back and watch the world go by.

Saturn/Neptune 3H
Helpful, understanding, sincere and wise are words that spring to mind when considering this aspect. The imagination (Neptune) is powerful but is kept under control (Saturn).

The Square or Fourth Harmonic (4H)

The square is probably one of the most difficult aspects to handle, but also one of the most beneficial when dealt with sensibly. Squares are the division of the circle by four, resulting in 90° wave lengths. The bodies in square to each other do not have very much in common and thus there is difficulty in working together. However, they do (usually) have like qualities and thus there is some base to begin co-operation.

Again, here are a few examples. I cannot stress too often that aspects, like everything else, must be blended into the full picture and not simply looked at alone.

Sun/Moon 4H

Since the Sun represents the natural self and therefore the natural resources and the Moon the instinctive emotions and desires, when these two bodies are square to each other, then the conscious and subconscious parts of the individual are at odds with each other. There will be difficulty in using the natural resources to fulfil the instinctive desires. The outcome very often is dissatisfaction and frustration. However, if this square can be used constructively by self-control and hard work within the limitations of resources, then the outcome will be emotional contentment, stemming from physical success.

Mercury/Mars 4H

Whenever these two planets connect (no matter what the aspect), there is always an abundance of mental (Mercury) energy (Mars). When the connection is the square, what appears to be lacking and has to be worked at is determination and perseverance. Both planets are great starters, always ready to investigate (Mercury) and initiate (Mars) new ideas (Mercury) and actions (Mars) – but both tend to tire and get bored very easily. What we have in essence, with a connection between these two, is the qualities of both Gemini and Aries combined. Gemini and Aries do work well together, and with effort, so can this aspect. Solid earthy connections from other areas of the chart are what is needed for it to be of greatest benefit.

Venus/Jupiter 4H
The ancient astrologers called these two planets the Lesser and Greater Benefic. Naturally, therefore, any connection between the two was considered beneficial. However, it has to be said that I have not found it so! Venus can be a very difficult planet when given too much of its own way – think of both the negative Taurean acquisitive and possessive characteristics and also the Libran manipulative bossy tendencies. Jupiter, too, has a very unsavoury side – its association with gambling for instance. When these two planets are square to each other, the negative side of both of them does seem to be exacerbated. However, the positive qualities of both planets are still there and, with effort, can be brought to the fore – the results being tremendously satisfactory (and quite often very remunerative).

The Sextile or Sixth Harmonic (6H)

The sixth harmonic is the division of the circle by six, giving wave lengths of 60°. Sextiles are medium-strength aspects and should not be allowed too wide an orb. If kept within strict limits of no more than 3°, they can prove very informative aspects, and can at times manifest themselves, if anything, stronger and more noticeably than 3H aspects.

Sextiles are traditionally beneficial, but the same warning as with the 3H applies. Too much of a good thing can be disastrous. It is said that the 6H indicates the potential of an individual. What it does *not* indicate is whether that potential will be achieved. Again, let's look at a few examples.

Sun/Saturn 6H
Depth of character, great understanding, and a capacity to help others is often indicated by a connection of these two planets (no matter what the aspect). Another outcome of traditionally easy aspects between the two is an indication of longevity, but this needs to be looked at carefully, in relation to the rest of the chart. The solid strength of Saturn is warmed and softened by contact with the Sun. The extrovert tendencies of the Sun, in turn, receive benefit from the quiet, ambitious tenacity of Saturn. The outcome is often success, at least on a worldly

level. Emotionally, Saturn can have a dampening effect on the normally optimistic Sun and pessimistic tendencies need to be consciously counteracted.

Moon/Mercury 6H

This aspect usually denotes a sensitive and thoughtful disposition. It can, however, manifest itself in two very different ways. If the Moon is the stronger planet, then the emotions will tend to colour the mental outlook, often clouding the issue. If Mercury is dominant, then the emotional nature may be subdued, due to too great an emphasis on logic. The rest of the chart needs to be examined to see which of these two outcomes is likely to apply. No matter which, a talent for communication is often indicative of this particular connection.

Venus/Neptune 6H

Creativity naturally stems from this aspect: Neptune endows an active imagination and Venus the ability to profit by it. Venus, in contact with Neptune, is rather softer than with Jupiter – the outcome is gentler and more compassionate. However, neither planet has much push by itself, as Neptune prefers to dream and Venus can be downright lazy. Therefore, strength is needed from other areas of the chart for the creative potential of this connection to be fulfilled.

The Quincunx (sometimes called Inconjunct) or (12H)

There are actually two twelfth harmonics – the semisextile (30° apart) and the inconjunct (150°, 30° from its polarity). Both aspects show an incompatibility between the bodies and both indicate strain. The inconjunct appears to be somewhat stronger in manifesting itself in an individual and can in fact be as difficult, if not more so, to handle than the square. Let's look at an example.

Sun/Uranus Inconjunct 12H

The strain and difficulty with this contact seems to revolve around co-operation with other people. Bitterness can be the outcome of yielding to other people's demands, simply because they expect it. At home or at work this aspect seems to indicate someone who is put-upon and used by others. What makes it worse is the Uranus is always anti-authoritarian and the Sun naturally likes to be in charge, yet the indications are that other people will be giving the orders. Tension and strain are the obvious outcome.

Summary of the Aspects

Understanding the planets is the key to correct interpretation of aspects. Remember Mars is always Mars; Jupiter always Jupiter, and so on. It is the qualities of the planets that are of greatest importance. The actual contact is secondary, but should, of course, always be kept in mind. Like a great many things in this very complex subject, practical application is the best teacher.

Chart analysis is complicated and involved. It has to be, for there are no more complex beings on earth than people!

The next chapters are devoted to the main purpose of this book: an explanation of astrological hereditary patterns. The reader is strongly advised to re-examine and fully understand these preliminary chapters before progressing further. If necessary, further guidance from other publications should be sought, in order to be assured of a good grounding in the basics of chart analysis before continuing with this work.

Family Tree

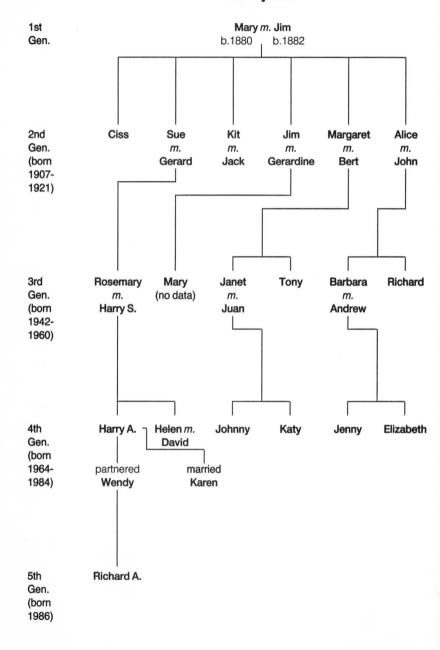

1st Gen.

Mary *m.* Jim
b.1880 b.1882

2nd Gen. (born 1907- 1921)

Ciss

Sue *m.* Gerard

Kit *m.* Jack

Jim *m.* Gerardine

Margaret *m.* Bert

Alice *m.* John

3rd Gen. (born 1942- 1960)

Rosemary *m.* Harry S.

Mary (no data)

Janet *m.* Juan

Tony

Barbara *m.* Andrew

Richard

4th Gen. (born 1964- 1984)

Harry A. ⌐ Helen *m.* David

partnered Wendy

Johnny

married Karen

Katy

Jenny

Elizabeth

5th Gen. (born 1986)

Richard A.

Chapter 6

Family Matters

A great many years ago a friend bought me a book on sun signs for Christmas. The lady in question was a Piscean and totally convinced that sun-sign astrology worked. I was not. Nevertheless, the book was written with style and in such a way as to be quite entertaining, so I thanked her and promised to read it from cover to cover. I did not start at the beginning but naturally enough turned to my own sun sign. I had to admit that, although I did not particularly fit the descriptions therein, my husband certainly did, at least in part. He did. I didn't. Why? Coincidence, probably. Still, my curiosity was aroused and I read on.

This time I jumped to Virgo, my young son's sign. Another blank. Neat, tidy? The author should see his bedroom! Hygienic? Interested in health? He certainly gave the impression that he thought he had an allergy to soap! As I thought in the first place, utter rubbish. Still I persisted because I had promised to read it all. My daughter's sign, Libra, proved nearer the mark, but was still not totally accurate. Nevertheless, I could recognize a great deal in the chapters on Libran children. Again, the question arose of why some people fitted and others didn't. Finally, I decided to start the book from page one, which I suppose I should have done in the first place. Within a page I had discovered another surprise. The first chapter on Aries seemed to fill in the missing pieces in my husband's character. I reread Taurus – yes, that was very like him, but so too was a great deal of Aries. I passed on to Gemini (the sun sign of both my parents).

I remember that day well, and my first inklings that this strange subject really could reveal something about the workings of human nature. I found the pages on Gemini interesting and fascinating. The descriptions fitted both my parents – my father slightly more than my mother – but both were recognizable. What was even more amazing was that I could have been reading about myself. I fitted the characteristics described almost perfectly. Even to the revelation that Geminians have a habit of reading a book from back to front or at least of starting in the middle!

It struck me that since I was an eight-month baby, had I arrived when expected I would have been born a Geminian. Had that anything to do with it? I had to find out more. I spent weeks searching through all the books the local library could supply on astrology and, finally, with much difficulty, I managed to work out my own birth chart. The Gemini content stood out, no wonder Taurus didn't get much of a look in! It was, I reasoned, only to be expected. After all, both my parents were Geminians. Naturally they had passed on these tendencies to me. However, both my husband and myself were Taurean – but neither of our children appeared to have any Taurean traits. The plot thickened.

Next I worked out the birth charts of my parents, my husband and both of my children. The results were not what I had expected. True, the hereditary connection between my own chart and that of my parents was very obvious. Not just the Gemini content, but the strong Aquarius in all three. The same, however, did not seem to be the case with myself and my husband and our children. There appeared to be very little in common between us. Both children did have some Taurus – our son had Jupiter, and our daughter, Saturn. Neither had any Aries, the Sun Ruler of both myself and my husband. Our daughter had no Gemini whatsoever and our son had it only on the Midheaven. I was bemused.

I was, however, beginning to be convinced that chart analysis worked or, at least, appeared to work. But was it simply the case that I was making it fit? If there was any truth in the subject, there had to be a recognizable hereditary link. We are genetically a 50/50 blend of our parents, and they in turn of theirs – therefore, I reasoned, the same thing should apply to our astrological make-up.

I had to investigate further and, indeed, for the last 15 years research and study has taken up a great deal of my time. Every time I appeared to have found a link, upon closer investigation (and when applied to a larger number of charts) it didn't hold up. I was sorely tempted not only to give up the search but also to revert to my original opinion of astrology, but somehow I couldn't. It did work. *It did!*

I contented myself with becoming more and more proficient and conversant with the ins and outs of the subject. I became a practising astrologer and discovered over and over again just how accurate birth-chart analysis could be. It showed the real person – not just the outer image the subject wanted to display.

Over the years I kept going back to my search for the 'missing link' and at last I found it. Like all discoveries, the answer had been staring me in the face all along, only it was so obvious that I had missed it, or rather misinterpreted it.

There are so many hereditary patterns that the sheer number of them tend to cloud the issue. It is like looking at the intricate pattern on a woven carpet, each colour and thread interwoven with its neighbour until all you see is the complete picture and in doing so you lose sight of the individual strands. What you have to do is start with one strand (or idea) and follow it through to its conclusion, ignoring any other interconnections along the way. Then the true make-up of the picture is revealed.

The First Strand

One of the first things I had noticed in my research was that the mother's Moon position seemed to interchange quite frequently with the offsprings' Ascendant. My own Ascendant is less than a degree away from exactitude from my mother's Moon. This occurs quite frequently but in itself is not enough to be considered a definite pattern. However, it occurred to me, that there was another slightly less frequent connection: that of the mother's Sun exchanging signs with the offspring's MC. Perhaps, the two occurrences were part of the same pattern.

I found the Midheaven placing particularly interesting because of the fact that although my daughter has Libra on the Ascendant like her father, they both have different Midheavens. My husband's MC is Leo (like his mother's Sun); and my daughter's is in Cancer (as I later realized, my Sun overlay and my mother's Sun Ruler!).

Usually, in Northern Hemispheres, when Libra is rising the MC is found in the sign of Cancer. There is only a small fraction of time when Libra Ascends that it falls in Leo. When I began to experiment with overlays as actual degrees in their own right (not merely house signs), I found that my son and daughter both have 28/29° Gemini as one of their Midheaven placings – his MC sign and her MC ruler overlay!

My son was born three weeks later than expected, and after I had been in labour for almost twenty-three hours. The doctor and midwife had decided that I was not going to manage the birth naturally and had sent for an ambulance to take me to hospital. It was a Monday morning and, both having surgeries or clinics to attend, they departed, leaving a trainee nurse in attendance to await the arrival of the ambulance. Suddenly, I knew the baby was coming.

'Don't push!' cried the nurse, quite panic-stricken. Too late! Into the world came my crinkled little baby. His hearty cry heralded his arrival just as the City Hall clock chimed eight hours. When I later worked out his birth chart, I found his Midheaven clinging on to the last minutes of Gemini. There was very little time left before both it and the Ascendant would have changed signs. I know with absolute certainty that after 23 hours of trying to force him into the world, we both knew exactly when the right moment had arrived.

Factors and Formula

From these first tentative conjectures the picture slowly began to emerge. There are three distinct but interconnecting factors on which the pattern evolves. They are:

1 Degrees of signs and overlays
2 Personal planets
3 Aspect harmonics

All three form part of our astrological hereditary patterns and interconnecting them all is a simple but consistent two-part dominant formula:

Sun/MC/Descendent and Moon/IC/Ascendant

More often than not, the connections follow this formula but sometimes they cross it, as with recessive features in genetics. Another interesting factor is that there seems to be a dominant and recessive way in which the formula works, depending upon whether it is coming from the maternal or paternal side. For instance, as mentioned before, the mother's Moon very often moves to the child's Ascendant and the mother's Sun to the child's MC. But the father's Moon or Ascendant are more likely to stay in their original placing in his offspring: so too the father's Sun. Sun and Descendent interchanges are more likely to skip a generation (grandparents to grandchildren), so too the Moon and IC. These are not hard and fast rules but do occur frequently enough to be called dominant features.

Let us examine the first two factors together in detail. The third aspect, harmonics, will be looked at separately in a later chapter. First, though, a reminder of what constitutes a personal planet.

There are six planets of major importance in everyone's chart (apart from the Sun and Moon). They are:

Chart Ruler	– planet ruling the Ascendant's sign
MC Ruler	– planet ruling the Midheaven's sign
Sun Ruler	– planet ruling the Sun's sign
Moon Ruler	– planet ruling the Moon's sign
Dec Ruler	– planet ruling the Descendent's sign
IC Ruler	– planet ruling the Nadir's sign

Do you remember how rulership works? To refresh your memory, each sign has a planet that is said to rule it. This planet is highly compatible with that particular sign. For example, the Sun is the obvious ruler of the sign of Leo.

The personal planets are worked out on this basis. If, for instance, the Ascendant is found in Libra and the Midheaven in Cancer, with Sun in Taurus and Moon in Scorpio, the following are the personal planets:

Chart Ruler:	Venus (Ruler of Libra)
MC Ruler:	Moon (Ruler of Cancer)
Sun Ruler:	Venus (Ruler of Taurus)
Moon Ruler:	Pluto (Ruler of Scorpio)
Descendent Ruler:	Mars (Ruler of Aries)
IC Ruler:	Saturn (Ruler of Capricorn)

It is important to remember both rulerships and personal planets as we work through the hereditary data. When looking at a particular point, there are always four placings to consider, for example, with the Sun: you would take the actual placing, the placing of the Sun's Ruler and the placings of the overlays of both; or with the Ascendant: the actual placing of the rising sign; its Ruler (the Chart Ruler) and the Ruler's overlay. The overlay of the Ascendant and Descendent is the same for everyone – 00° Aries and 00° Libra, therefore as a hereditary factor they are ignored.

At the back of this work you will find the full astrological data for the examples used in the rest of this book. It spans a whole century and five generations from Mary and Jim, a couple born in the 1880s, through to their great-great-grandson, Richard, born in 1986.

To make the examples more interesting and to avoid the boredom of reading through page after page of astrological tables, I shall attempt to let the reader learn about the hereditary patterns by studying the people themselves. In doing so, I also hope that some of the astrological analysis, explained in the earlier chapters, will become clearer and that the reader will see how informative astrology can be in explaining the substance and anomalies of human nature.

For convenience, I will abbreviate the following:

Ascendant to Asc
Descendent to Dec
Midheaven to MC
Nadir to IC
Sun to Sn
Moon to Mn
Overlay to Ovl

where a rulership is involved, I will simply add an 'R' at the end. For example ChR = Chart Ruler (Ruler of the Asc).

The First Generation

Mary, a sun-sign Geminian, was born in Greenock, Scotland, of a Scottish father and an Irish mother. She was brought up according to the strict rules of the Roman Catholic faith and was a very pious person. Indeed, the whole family was steeped in religion and four of her five brothers became monks. Her Piscean MC and the Sagittarian overlay of Saturn (the ruler of both her Moon and her Descendent), help to explain this side of her nature. She grew up within the confines of a large but closely-knit Victorian family and thus home and family were very close to her heart (Cancer Asc).

On reaching adulthood, Mary married a young man, Jim, from the same town as herself. To outsiders she appeared the epitomy of a gentle, quiet, submissive wife, but this was not altogether the case. True, she was mindful of her duties and was naturally mild and gentle, but there was a quiet, magnetic force about her (Scorpio MC Ovl), and a dogged determination (strong Taurus content) that was not always outwardly apparent. As a matter of fact, it was she, and not her dominant husband, who greatly influenced her children.

Her astrological mix was very varied. Her Sun lay in Gemini, as did its Ruler, Mercury; both had Aquarius as overlay (all air signs). Her Moon lay in Capricorn with Virgo as overlay (both earth signs); her Moon Ruler, Saturn, was in Aries and had Sagittarius for overlay (both fire signs). Her Ascendant was Cancer and her Midheaven Pisces (both water). So you see all four elements were evenly distributed. This distribution of elements would normally indicate a balanced personality, and to some extent it did. But there was one area where an imbalance appeared in her make-up. Unfortunately it was this imbalance which was to have a great effect upon her children.

She was a practical (all three earth signs) adaptable and agile-minded person (Gemini). She put her family first (Cancer Asc) and was naturally dutiful both to her husband and her faith (Pisces MC). She had Pisces as overlay to her Cancerean Mars, which combined with the strong Taurus content of her chart, should have indicated a physically sexy lady – but she wasn't! Or at least that was the impression given to her five daughters.

Mary had some very peculiar ideas (at least to the enlightened attitude of our generation) about this most taboo of subjects. In fact, her rather odd outlook towards it caused at least one of her daughters to develop an abnormal attitude to sex.

The Aquarian overlays of her Geminian Sun and Mercury go part of the way towards explaining her dislike of the physical. This combined with her naturally pious nature, when applied to the teachings of the Roman Catholic faith with regards to women and sex, must have exacerbated the problem. To complicate matters further, her husband was a particularly physical man (Sun and Mars in Scorpio – both by sign and overlay, and a very strong Taurus content in his chart). I have the feeling that she, too, could be sexually aroused but that it left her feeling dirty, guilty and sinful. After all, she had been brought up to believe that sexual enjoyment was for men only and was totally unnatural to womankind! Her Capricorn Moon with its Virgo overlay instinctively required her to conform to the expected norm.

None of her daughters were given any information about the workings of their bodies (periods came as a terrible shock!) and they were instructed that sexual feelings or thoughts were sinful. Sex was something which within a marriage was for the enjoyment of the husband and the endurance of the wife. At least one of them married without knowing the facts of life and the resultant shock, when coupled with the 'sinful' teachings of her mother, left her physically frigid. The other four girls also had hang-ups where 'the marriage bed' was concerned.

As a wife (remembering the age in which she was born), Mary saw it as her duty to go on producing children in rapid succession, year after year. She was married in June 1906 and in March 1907 her first child was born, followed in June 1908 by her second. In August 1909 she had her third child and in November 1910, her fourth. She then had two miscarriages, followed in September 1914 by the birth of a fifth child. World War 1 intervened, causing a gap in the production cycle. At the end of 1919 she gave birth to a still-born infant and in January 1921 her last child was born.

Physically, she was a tiny, rather frail lady (Asc Cancer:

Gemini/Aquarius Sun/overlay), yet four of her children weighed over ten pounds at birth. In those days there was no such thing as gas and air, let alone epidurals. The strain of her constant pregnancies finally took their toll. Whilst still in her fifties she was stricken by thrombosis and had to have a leg amputated. Not long after this tremendous shock to her system, tragedy struck when her only son was killed. She never really recovered from this blow, although she lived for several more years. Then thrombosis struck again, this time a coronary from which she died at the age of only 63 years.

Now let us take a look at her husband.

Jim had a dominant and forceful character, but with a delightfully charming personality (Sun Scorpio; Moon Taurus; with Venus in Libra). His true nature was in fact less strong than the general impression given. He had the sign of Capricorn on the Ascendant – in the Northern Hemisphere this is a sign of short ascension, which means that it is a reasonably rare occurrence. When Capricorn rises, I have found that something about the early life tends to be difficult and that the child more often than not is brought up in a family beset by difficult circumstances. This was, in fact, true of Jim.

His father, a journeyman joiner, had gone to sea as a ship's carpenter because of the lack of employment in his home town. A young wife and two small sons were left to fend for themselves for months on end. After an accident on board ship, he lost both his arm and his job. His wife had to take on the responsibility for the family and found employment as a lady's maid. Not only did she support her two sons, but she saw to it that they got the education needed to give them a better start in life.

This love of education, and the need for it as a means of security, was passed on to Jim. He in his turn was to see to it that his children's education took priority. His MC was in the sign of Sagittarius (the sign most associated with higher education).

He ruled his family with the proverbial rod of iron and his word was law. Anything he disapproved of was automatically banned. Even as his family matured, he maintained a firm grip on what they could or could not do. He was immensely proud of his children and wanted them all to do well in life. He knew what was best for them and they were obliged to follow his guidelines. They were not allowed to develop their own ideas or follow their own inclinations. The Taurus, Scorpio and Capricorn elements within him combined to create this rigidity. The eldest children suffered most from this severe attitude. By the time his youngest child was born, he was beginning to mellow and she was allowed a freedom of movement never bestowed upon the others. The unfairness of this treatment led to resentment from at least two of his children.

Jim had distinguished himself during World War 1 and volunteered on the outbreak of World War 2, only to be told that he was too old. After this rejection he suddenly retired from a promising and successful career at the very early age of 44, saying that he wanted to have more time to spend with his wife and growing family. But he was a restless person and enjoyed travelling (Sagittarius MnR and MC) and she was a 'home bird' (Cancer Asc). He therefore went off on 'jaunts' without her, usually with an old army buddy. The deterioration in Mary's health finally put a stop to his globe-trotting. After she lost her leg, he devoted himself to taking care of her. When their son died so tragically, although grief-stricken himself, he did his best to comfort and console his wife. But there was little he could do and helplessly he watched her health fade.

After Mary's death Jim remarried, just ten short months later. He did so both for companionship and physical contact (the Libra, Scorpio and Taurus mix of his make-up). Unfortunately his second wife had none of the qualities of his first. The apparently strong and dominating man soon faded to a shadow of his former self, quickly becoming a pale, weak, hen-pecked husband. Within a year he, too, was dead.

Mary and Jim were both emotionally motivated people; both had water signs strongly placed, she Asc, he Mn overlay and MCR, in Cancer. She also had Pisces as her MC sign, whilst his Sun lay in Scorpio. This strong water content was passed on to all their children, as we shall see.

One of the most dominant signs in the charts of both was that of Taurus. Mary had it as IC at 25° 35′ and as MCR at 12° 42′;

Jim had Mn (his DecR and MnOvR) at 09° 51' and ChR/ SnOvR at 24° 11' and SnR 29° 36'. How then was this sign passed on to their six children: Ciss, Sue, Kit, Jim, Margaret and Alice?

Ciss, the eldest, had 25° 55' Taurus as her IC Ovl (very close to her mother's). Sue also had Taurus as her IC Ovl but at 18° 17' (quite close to her father's ChR and very close to his Neptune 17° 47' – Neptune was her Sn OvlR: Kit had 17° 58' Taurus as her Mn sign. The only boy, Jim A., had it as IC Ovl at 26° 31', and also as DecR but the degree 01° 59' is rather wide and not in line with the dominant formula. Margaret had Venus Ovl at 09° 56' (very close to her father's Mn – Venus was his MnR). Alice, the youngest, did not have the sign at all. However, the sign does appear strongly, and with close connections to her parents' placings, in the charts of both her children.

You see how the placings move (generally within the formula) between signs, overlays and rulers. Note how close some of these connections are. We will follow this sign further as we progress through the generations. In the next chapter we will examine the lives and characters of the children – the second generation of our example family.

Chapter 7

The Second Generation

The Eldest Child

Ciss, a gentle sweet-natured person, lived in a world of her own. She loved to pretend and later on to act and make up her own stories and plays. She was also musically inclined (Pisces Sn and Mn). However, there was a serious and ambitious side to her nature (Sn in conjunct aspect (1H) with the MC). She was academically minded and achieved, with ease, an honours degree before becoming a teacher, a job she thoroughly enjoyed. The strong religious devotion inherited from her mother and shown by the dominance of Pisces (and Sagittarius from her father) in her chart eventually led to her becoming a nun. The order she joined was a teaching one and she remained immersed in her profession until her mental faculties were impaired by a series of strokes. She died in her early sixties from the final massive one.

The tremendous domination of the water signs in Ciss's chart caused a serious imbalance. She had all three in prominent positions and this affected every part of her make-up. Like her mother she had a Cancer Asc but in her case the Moon as ChR lay in close 1H conjunct aspect to her Piscean Sun, both having a Sagittarius Ovl. Her MC too had this same combination, her ICR (Mercury) also lay in Pisces again with Sagittarius as Ovl; her DecR Saturn was also in Pisces, but this time with a Scorpio Ovl. Her SnR, MnR and MCR (Neptune) was in Cancer with a Pisces Ovl. How emotionally motivated can you get? Her birth chart indicated that she really was not equipped to face the rough and tumble of this world, despite her driving ambition and academic prowess.

The Second Child

At just 15 months younger than her sister, Sue couldn't have been more different. Like her mother she had a Geminian Sn. The Sn Ovl in her chart was Pisces, but she had four planets, including her SnR, with an Aries Ovl. Sue was a fighter!

From an obstinate, but rather shy youngster (Cancer Asc with Aquarius MC and Mn), she grew into a forthright and headstrong adult. She did not marry until she was in her mid-thirties and had no wish to 'tie herself down' before that (Aquarius Mn). She married a man six years her junior, and eighteen months later gave birth to their only child, a daughter.

Sue became a teacher like her sister and was particularly suited for the profession. It was not the career she would have chosen for herself as it was imposed upon her by her father. However, the ability to teach was in-born and her pupils benefited from this natural talent (Jupiter in Leo). Her life was full of ups and downs, often caused by her own disposition, for she was highly-strung and suffered from nervous disorders such as dermatitis (Capricorn-ruled Aquarian Moon coupled with a Gemini Sun and the strong Cancerian element).

She lived into her mid-eighties. Until the last two or three years she was an extremely active, young-at-heart individual (Gemini sun sign; Aries overlays). Her mind, always keen and sharp, remained alert to the end, but the minor forgetfulness and slight confusion that did occur in the later years troubled her greatly and she became obsessed with the fear of losing her mind. (The Scorpio Ovl of both her Moon and MC accounted for some of this obsession, together with the natural worrying tendency of the extremely strong Cancer element of her make-up exacerbating the situation.)

She never learned to accept the limitations of old age (a very badly aspected Saturn in Aries) and because of this her last few years were very unhappy indeed. She felt useless and unloved and became permanently depressed (the strong Capricorn/Cancer content). Nothing could lift her spirits. Capricorn can be a very heavy sign, particularly when associated with the Moon – a connection she had inherited from her mother.

Mary's Mn/ChR was 26° 41' Capricorn, close to her Dec at 28° 58': she also had Venus (strong in its own sign of Taurus) on Ov 25° 21' Capricorn. Jim's Asc was 29° 19', his Sn Ovl 11° 15' and his ICR Ovl 01° 19' Capricorn. This combination of placements meant that this sign would permeate both sides of the hereditary formula in their children. Let us see just how it passed on.

Ciss had Dec 24° 17' (very close to her mother's). Sue also had Dec in this sign – but at 4° 22' closer to her father's placings. From a grandparent perhaps? She also had Uranus (MnR) at 20° 02' quite close to her mother's Moon and very close to her father's Asc. The Moon was her mother's ChR. Uranus was her MCR. Her DecR Ovl lay at 4° 50' (her DecR is Saturn – her mother's MnR).

Kit had ChR Ovl at 05° 06' (close to Sue's Dec and Saturn Ovl, which adds to the 'evidence' that this area of Capricorn came from grandparents). Jim A., like his eldest sister, Ciss, had Dec at 25° 20' and DecR Ovl (Saturn) at 06° 39' (that same vicinity again!). Margaret did not have the sign as a personal placing but once again it is her Saturn Ovl. Alice had it as Sn Ovl, 21° 00', and MC, 06° 39' (exactly the same as her brother's Saturn Ovl!).

Later we will re-examine this sign as it passes through further generations. Let us for the moment, however, return to the second child of the second generation.

Sue died from an accident at the age of 84. Apparently she fell down the stairs in the early hours of the morning; nobody will ever know the full details of what happened. It is astrologically significant that she should have met her end in such a way, for at her birth Mercury (the ruler of her Gemini Sun) lay in close conjunction (01' orb 1H) with Mars (the ruler of Mercury's overlay). Accidents were always on the cards and this accident and her subsequent death highlight the significance of the four personal points in a birth chart. Her Ascendant was the sign of Cancer – the sign that rules the home. The Mercury and Mars conjunction mentioned above also lay in that sign (the home being the place where the accident occurred). During the fall, she sustained multiple fractures (bones are ruled by the sign of Capricorn – her Descendent). Death actually occurred because her heart was unable to cope with the internal bleeding caused by the fractures – the heart is ruled by Leo (her IC) and the circulation by Aquarius (her MC sign).

On the day of her death the planet Uranus (her MCR and MnR) had returned exactly to the point of the zodiac where it was at her birth – in opposition (2H) to that fatal conjunction of Mars and Mercury and Square (4H) to Saturn!

The Third Child

Kit was born a sun-sign Leo, less than 14 months after Sue. You will remember that when the Sun falls in Leo it is reinforced in strength because the Sun is the ruler of Leo. Leo was her father's IC Ovl (09° 47′) and ChR/Sn Ovr (01° 52′ Ovl) but this is a bit wide – Kit's Sn lay at 15° 26′.

From the start, Kit tended to speak her mind and she could certainly 'flare' when crossed (Sagittarius Asc and Mars in its own sign of Aries!). Since all three fire signs were strong in her make-up, she was naturally a *very* warm person who was also generous to a fault. However, there was a darker side to her nature. She was born in the shadow of her two elder sisters. Both the older girls were highly intelligent, Ciss having ability and ambition while Sue was mentally bright, physically athletic and possessed a gregarious personality. Both girls were pretty.

Kit had a somewhat sluggish personality and less mental agility. That is not to say that she was backward, for although she was not as mentally quick as her sisters, she did have sound common sense. Her Taurus Moon and ChR Ovl Capricorn probably accounted for this. She was also physically less attractive than they were. It must have seemed to her from the start that the odds were stacked against her – and indeed so it seemed to be. Life from beginning to end let her down!

She was the first child in the family to inherit a strong Virgo content in her chart. Ciss had it on the IC but, in her case, it was overpowered by the very strong Pisces content of her make-up. Sue did not have any Virgo content at all. Kit, on the other hand, had Virgo as Mn Ovl (04° 51′); MnR/MCR 12° 58′ and ChR 18° 13′. Thus, this most difficult of signs, was found in both halves of her chart. Where did it come from?

Mary had IC at 27° 33', Mn/ChR Ovl at 27° 43' and Uranus at 04° 58' (Uranus is the ruler of Aquarius, which was the Ovl of her Sn and SnR/ICR). Jim had Virgo (09° 00') as MCR Ovl.

Why it should be that Virgo seems to bring its own 'cross to bear' to those who have it featured strongly in their charts I really do not know (perhaps it is in the very 'nature of the beast') – but there is no doubt that such is the case! Virgo is a difficult enough sign to handle when it takes its positive form, but when (as in Kit's case) it takes on its negative one, then life can be pretty unbearable for all concerned.

Her life was dogged by frustrations. In the early years she felt inferior to her elder sisters – not a feeling conducive to a Leo sun sign, nor for that matter for the Sagittarius and Aries content of her make-up. None of the fire signs are happy being relegated to anything other than 'top spot'. Her Leo Sn (Sagittarius Ovl) was in 4H Square aspect to her Taurus Moon (Virgo Ovl). Remember that this aspect nearly always causes frustrations and set-backs for the individual.

As she grew up, ill-health troubled her and interfered with her schooling, thus, we shall never know if she was capable of achieving the standards set by her sisters. Because of this, it was assumed that she should be the one elected (or selected by fate) to remain at home and take care of her parents as they grew older. But Kit had other ideas (Sagittarius Asc!), and set about the task of finding herself a suitable husband in the most methodical and meticulous manner (Taurus and Virgo combined). Eventually – she was the last of the family to marry – she found a suitable partner. But all was not to be as she'd intended.

Not long after they were married it was discovered that her husband was suffering from tuberculosis. He was obliged to give up his thriving business (he owned a barber's shop) and she had to take on the role of provider (like her paternal grandmother before her). On top of this, although she longed for children (Leo Sun), motherhood was denied her. During the 15 years of her marriage – before consumption claimed her husband's life – she never conceived.

It says a lot for the warmth and generosity of spirit of Kit's fire signs that she never let the bitterness she felt totally consume her. Optimistically, to the bitter end, she waited for her ship to come home – *it never did!*

She died alone in her flat after suffering a heart attack (Leo content), mistakenly believing that she had called a doctor, when in fact all she had spoken to was an answerphone! Neptune, the planet of illusion, which was very badly aspected in her chart, was certainly at work that night.

The Fourth Child

We now come to the only boy to be born alive. Jim A., like Ciss, had his Asc very close to his mother's at 25° 20′ Cancer. The water signs were very strong in him (Scorpio Sun, Venus, Mars and Jupiter; Cancer Asc; Pisces MC; and water signs as overlays), thus he was a gentle, sensitive boy. As a youngster he was mollycoddled by his mother and as he grew, in the shadow of a dominant father and surrounded by five sisters, he did not develop his true potential. However, with the advent of World War 2 he suddenly found himself in a different environment – His Majesty's Forces. He blossomed. The weak and sickly boy became a man.

He threw off the physical disabilities of his childhood (real or imagined) and mentally, physically and emotionally found himself (Leo Moon and Sn Ovl). Before long he met and married and later a daughter was born. Then tragedy struck: Jim was killed in an accident.

The circumstances of his death, although occurring years before and happening a long way from home, were not dissimilar to Sue's death – both involved falls and multiple fractures. His SnR, Pluto, lay on 27° 26′ Gemini – close to her Sun at 26° 25′ Gemini; her Sun Ovl on 22° 02′ Pisces lay almost on the same degree as his MC at 21° 51′ Pisces; her Mars (the planet usually associated with accidents and injuries to the head) was on 17° 07′ Cancer, whilst his Mars Ovl was 15° 38′ Cancer. A lot more coincidences occur in their charts.

The Fifth Child

Margaret's chart, like that of Kit's, had a strong Virgo content and like her sister she was destined to endure cruel twists of fate throughout her life. Unlike her sister she did not have the warmth of Leo to aid and abet her. Both Aries and Sagittarius are in her chart, but these are counteracted by the water signs in her make-up (Pisces Sn Ovl and Dec with DecR Cancer). The water signs, as we have already discovered, are all emotionally motivated, but Virgo – the most dominant sign in her chart (Asc; Sn; ChR; SnR; MCR) – smothers the emotions and keeps them hidden; a difficult combination indeed. How she coped with it we will see.

As a youngster she was quiet and introverted, with large clear grey eyes, which very often indicates the presence of Virgo in a person. She was born in 1914 just at the outbreak of World War 1, thus it was that for the first few years of her life her father was absent. Suddenly, when she was just four years old, he swept into her life, and turned it upside-down!

Her father had distinguished himself during the war and had gained the respect and life-long friendship of a senior officer whose life he had saved. After the war, in recognition of this, the officer provided both home and civilian job for him. However, it meant having to leave Scotland and the whole family was uprooted and moved to the industrial north of England.

Margaret grew into an attractive and charming young woman (the Libra inherited from her father). She married a young man (Libra sun sign) who absolutely adored her. He was sent overseas within days of their wartime wedding and she was not to see him again for over five years.

After his return they lived happily together and all was well, except for the fact that she did not seem able to have children. Several miscarriages occurred but no completed pregnancies. Then, 15 years after they married, and as she approached her fortieth birthday, a daughter was born. This was followed a year later by the arrival of a son. The couple were overjoyed!

The upheaval of becoming a mother at this late stage in life was very upsetting and she found herself unable to cope with the pressures it put upon her (strong Pisces overlay; just beginning to make itself felt as she reached the menopause). She began to let herself go and her husband became disillusioned when he found his idol had feet of clay. (Typical Libra sun-sign reaction.)

The early years of the children's lives were very difficult ones for her. Her husband was a marvellous father who both enjoyed and idolized his children. The difficult years passed and the youngsters approached their teens – then suddenly the world fell apart. Their son was taken ill and died within a matter of days. They were devastated. Margaret, in true Virgo fashion, hid her anguish beneath an appearance of calm acceptance. Her husband never really got over the loss. Their daughter became the centre of her parents' world. But she (as we will see later) had an independent spirit and had been born with itchy feet. As soon as she was able, she left home and set out on her travels, leaving behind broken-hearted parents.

Not long after their daughter had left, Margaret awoke one morning to find her husband dead in bed beside her! Life at that moment must have seemed to have come to an end for her too. Her husband and son were dead and her only daughter was far away at the other side of the world! She was not to die, however, but was to live on alone for many years. She is now in her late seventies and all her sisters are gone. She is a quiet, sad, resigned and rather helpless old lady.

There may yet be hope on the horizon for her. Her daughter, now married and living in Mexico, has asked her to go and live with them. Perhaps, just perhaps, she may yet find the happiness which has eluded her for so long.

The Sixth Child

We now come to the last of the six children: Alice, a pretty, vain, and thoroughly spoiled daughter who was born almost 14 years after the eldest child, Ciss. Over the years their father, in particular, had mellowed with age. His attitude towards his youngest child was very different to that experienced by his other children. This naturally caused a certain resentment towards her on their part.

Alice's astrological mix well demonstrates the potentially disastrous coming together of the signs Scorpio and Aquarius. She had an Aquarian Sun and a Scorpio Moon – not the easiest of combinations. Where did they come from? Mary had Sn Ovl in Aquarius and also SnR/ICR Ovl; she had MC Ovl in Scorpio. Jim's Sn was in Scorpio as was his MCR Ovl, and he also had Mars in that sign (Mars was Alice's ChR!); he had Aquarius as MC Ovl and MnR Ovl.

To understand the problems of merging two such diverse signs we need to re-examine each separately. Aquarius is an erratic highly-strung sign, which has an unemotional, friendly but detached attitude to other people. It is also rather asexual in make-up. Scorpio on the other hand – as has been so well documented – is highly sexed and intensely emotional. However, these strong emotions are kept hidden by the deeply secretive nature. It is also an extremely jealous and possessive sign. Thus, as you can imagine, the two signs are not at all compatible and when they appear together in a person the tension created can be catastrophic.

Alice began life as a pretty, happy, active youngster. From the very beginning her mother recognized both the strengths and weaknesses of her 'baby'. She was self-centred and vain but she also had great strength of character. (She had Asc at 19° 00' Aries.) Her mother called Alice, her 'Scarlet O'Hara' – the best fictional example of Aries characteristics; both good and bad.

She married early, at just 19 years of age, the strongly romantic Libra element in her combining with self-deluding Pisces, headstrong Aries and anti-authority (you'll not tell me!) Aquarius. The marriage was not destined to be a happy one. The warning signs had been clear for all to see. Throughout their courtship the couple had quarrelled ceaselessly and bitterly. It seemed they could not live together in harmony, yet found it impossible to live apart. From this dark, brooding and potentially violent relationship came forth two children, a daughter and a son (12 years later).

When her daughter was born, the possessive nature of Alice's Scorpio Moon consumed her. She cut off from her affections every other human being, including her husband, and lived totally for her daughter. Her husband was not even allowed to correct the child, let alone show her any love! Her sisters were admonished for trying to share the affections of the little girl. She belonged to her and her alone! The outcome of this unnatural Scorpio extreme was obvious disaster for all concerned.

Her husband, a depressive and moody man to begin with (SnR Cancer; Moon Capricorn), cut off from his wife and daughter's affections, became morose and miserable. He took it out on his wife by punishing the whole family with long moody silences. The atmosphere within the home was incredible. As their daughter began to grow up, she found it both smothering and depressive. Academic studies offered her a way out, and gratefully she took it.

Then another baby arrived on the scene – the son his father had always longed for! But his birth brought no more happiness than had the birth of his sister. With the passing years the inevitable happened – both children grew away from their parents.

The fearful pressures that had been exerted on both partners within this unhappy relationship began to take their toll. Her husband developed angina and Alice suffered a complete mental and physical breakdown. With a badly aspected Aquarian Sun, this had always been a possibility.

She was not prepared to give in though (Aries Asc) and fought her way back to normality. Physically, the tremendous inner tensions had resulted in a terrible legacy, for she discovered she was terminally ill. How she faced up to this discovery and conducted what remained of her life showed the tremendous strength of character she possessed (Aries Asc; Capricorn MC; Scorpio Moon). Although physically very weak, she set about putting her affairs in order (Capricorn on the MC). Up to that point in time, her life may have been vain and selfish, but in its closing stages she showed a tenacious and courageous spirit that few could have matched. All who knew her could not help but admire the lady!

Before moving on to the next chapter and another generation, I would like to examine further some of the hereditary connections between the first and second generations. There are far too many to examine them all and we have already looked at several. I will take just one example from each parent. The mother's Moon and the father's Sun. Remember, when looking at a particular placing, you must also take into account the ruler by planet and sign and all respective overlays.

Mother's Moon:

Moon sign 26° 41' Capricorn; Moon overlay 27° 43' Virgo
MnR sign 24° 38' Aries; MnR Ovl 25° 40' Sagittarius
The relevant planets are Saturn, the ruler of Capricorn, and Mars, the ruler of Aries.

We should also take into account Mercury (ruler of Virgo) and Jupiter (ruler of Sagittarius) by both sign and overlay, if we wanted to find the complete hereditary picture as far as the Moon is concerned. For our present purpose, however, the above four placings will suffice as examples.

Father's Sun:

Sun sign 03° 34' Scorpio; Sun overlay 11° 15' Capricorn
SnR sign 29° 36' Taurus; SnR Ovl 07° 17' Leo
The relevant planet in this case is Pluto, the ruler of Scorpio and Saturn, the ruler of Capricorn.

Again, we could look at Venus, the ruler of Taurus, and Sun, the ruler of Leo, for the full break-down, but so long as we keep these in mind, we can make do with the above.

Now let us look at the six children.

Ciss:

IC 20° 12' Virgo (from mother's Mn Ovl)
IC Ovl 25° 55' Taurus (from father's SnR)
DecR Ovl 24° 01' Scorpio (from mother's MC Ovl)

Sue:

MnR 20° 02' Capricorn (from mother's Mn)
Dec 04° 226' and DecR Ovl 04° 50' Capricorn (from father's Sn Ovl)

Kit:
IC 20° 49' Aries (from mother's MnR)
Saturn 23° 13' Aries (from mother's MnR)
MC OvR 17° 59' and ChR/Sn OvR 05° 06' Capricorn (from father's Sn Ovl); Sn 15° 26' and Saturn 10° 06' Leo (from father's SnR Ovl)

Jim:
Mn/ChR Ovl 22° 53' Aries (from mother's MnR)
IC Ovl 26° 31' Taurus (from father's ChR); Mn OvR 10° 58' Scorpio (from father's Sn); Saturn (DecR) Ovl 06° 39' Capricorn (from father's Sn Ovl); Sn Ovl 04° 18' Leo (from father's SnR Ovl)

Margaret:
ChR 20° 32' Virgo (from mother's Mn Ovl)
MnR Ovl 25° 31' Aries (from mother's MnR)
Pluto Ovl 05° 25' Scorpio (from father's Sn); Saturn Ovl 11° 18' Capricorn (from father's Sn Ovl)

Alice:
Asc 19° 00' Aries (from mother's MnR)
Saturn 24° 13' Virgo (from mother's Mn Ovl)
Mn 05° 05' Scorpio (from father's Sn); MC 06° 39' Capricorn (from father's Sn Ovl)

There are many more connections to be found using the same method. The above serves to demonstrate how the formula works (dominant on the whole; not always!), and it shows the interconnection between rulers, signs and overlays.

Hereditary patterns will be traced further in the next chapter, as we look at the lives and characters of the third generation.

Postscript
Since the compilation of this book, Margaret, the last remaining member of this generation, has died. She did get to Mexico and spent a few brief but happy weeks there with her family. She died, no longer alone, but content and happy with her daughter and grandchildren.

Chapter 8

The Third Generation

The third generation consists of five cousins, three girls and two boys. In the case of the first grandchild, Rosemary (Sue's daughter), we not only have the full maternal data but also the partial data of her paternal grandparents and the 'rectified' data of her father. This fills in the picture in much greater detail than with the other four children. In their case only partial data (without times) of the fathers are known. Nevertheless, it can be seen in all five how the hereditary formula moves through this generation. Some of the degrees found are significantly closer between grandparents and grandchildren than those found between parents and children – this is often the case. Perhaps this explains the close relationship often experienced between these relatives.

The First Grandchild

Rosemary arrived in the world a full month before she was expected. The sun was at 24° 33' Taurus at the moment of her birth. Venus, you will remember, is the ruler of Taurus and a cursory look at her grandparents' charts reveals that her grandmother had Venus at 24° 19' Taurus (strong in its own sign), whilst her grandfather also had SnR on 29° 36' ChR/Sn OvlR at 24° 11' of this sign. The astrological significance of her unexpected arrival is clear.

Rosemary was a bright toddler, who gave every indication to her parents of great achievements to come. She began talking (fluently and clearly) at a very early age and had, it seemed, a phenomenal memory (Mercury in Gemini). At under two years of age she could recognize not only the main colours but could correctly identify shades and hues such as scarlet and vermilion, burgundy, beige, lavender, lilac, navy blue, bottle green, etc. She was also fluent with the names of garden flowers and plants (her father was a professional gardener) for which she had a great affection (Sun in Taurus). Names like Pyrethrum, Margarites and Antirrhinum rolled off her young tongue. Her parents were both amazed and delighted with their potential genius, but disappointment lay ahead.

The first indication that anything was wrong was when she attended preschool. While still being her bright, entertaining and friendly self, she nevertheless seemed to be at odds with her classmates. Even at this very early age, she didn't fit the mould. A dislike of conformity, beginning slowly in infancy, grew with the years, to become an antagonistic attitude towards the accepted 'norm' and the authorities who represent it (Aquarius Asc).

On top of this difficult attitude, she had another problem which was never envisaged in the brilliant early years – she was dyslexic. In those days, however, no such disability was recognized and she was simply classed as 'intellectually slow'. The frustrations of those years are still a vivid and disturbing memory to her. The combination of dyslexia and her attitude meant that although she managed to pass her 11+, she did not achieve a great deal at grammar school. It was not until she reached her mid thirties that she achieved anything substantial academically (Sagittarian MC opposed by Mercury in Gemini, itself conjunct (1H) to Jupiter.)

Despite the dyslexia, she loved books, and classical literature in particular, poetry and Shakespeare being great favourites. Alone in her room, away from the mockery of her classmates or parents, she was an avid reader. To this day she has difficulty in reading aloud in the presence of others – the mortification of stumbling over every word still lingers! Nevertheless, despite the problem she developed a love of drama and in time joined a drama society (Leo overlay of a Mercury/Jupiter conjunction – Mercury being not only her MnR and ICR but also her Final Dispositor and Jupiter being her MCR). Because of her reading difficulty she developed the skill of learning whole plays off by heart (even Shakespearean ones). Then, knowing them word for word, she could attend an audition without fear. This phenomenal feat did not seem out of the ordinary to her and it was only as she grew older (and the fear of being laughed at for her disability faded somewhat) that she began to appreciate her own worth (Saturn in Gemini conjunct (1H) not only both her Taurean Sun and Geminian Moon, but also in almost an exact conjunction (1H) to Uranus – her ChR).

She began 'scribbling' – writing stories and poems from a very early age; not that she showed the finished efforts to others very often because her 'atrocious spelling' (teacher Mum's words!) only caused them to laugh at her efforts. With the years – and the advent of word processors – this problem has abated somewhat and to this day she loves nothing better than to lose herself in her writings.

The Second Grandchild

The next grandchild to arrive was Barbara (Alice's daughter). She was a chubby 'Mabel Lucy Atwell' baby with large deep blue eyes, and particularly attractive, at least to look at! Her adoring mother ruined her, for she was spoiled rotten. Alice could see no wrong, no imperfection, no fault whatsoever in her 'little darling'. In her words, 'Barbara cannot even tell a lie!' What bunkum!

She was born with the Sun in Pisces and a strong Leo content in her chart, so even if her untruths were simply Piscean day dreams, or Leo exaggerations, they were still lies. She was a clever child (Mercury in Aquarius with Uranus in Gemini) and naturally ambitious (Capricorn Moon). Her father – although never allowed by her over-possessive mother to get emotionally close to his daughter – nevertheless endowed her with the will to achieve academic success as a means to future security.

The environment of her home life was unhappy, for she was smothered by her mother and distanced from her father. His constant moodiness and periods of brooding silence, combined with violent aggressive outbursts, made life quite intolerable. She threw herself into her studies, spending long hours at the library immersed in her books. When she got a place at university a new way of life opened up before her. Having once escaped from the constrictive confines of her mother's possessiveness, Barbara had no intention of allowing herself to be drawn back into her control (Jupiter in Sagittarius). A dreadful rift opened up as a result because Alice could not let her daughter go.

Years of isolation from her mother's love was the outcome for Barbara, who had done nothing worse than demand to be allowed to live her own life. What started as an all-consuming mother love, began to eat away at Alice. The gap between them became a chasm into which she eventually fell, overcome by mental illness. Whilst still in the throes of this illness, physical problems assailed Alice, who became a very sick lady. During this dreadful time, her husband's health gave out and he died of a heart attack. It is to their daughter's great credit that despite all the bitterness and unhappiness caused her by her parents, she never stopped loving them (Pisces Sn; Cancer Ovl) and that in her mother's final illness, she took her into her own home and cared for her. How many daughters given the same background, would have done so, I wonder. This is an example of Scorpio (Barbara's Asc) working at its positive and caring best, unfortunately not the face it very often shows the world.

The Third and Fourth Grandchildren

The third grandchild to arrive, long after the death of both grandparents, was Janet (Margaret's daughter), followed the next year by her brother, Tony. Both children arrived late in their parents' lives. They were normal active youngsters, although in some respects closer than a lot of brothers and sisters. Janet, being only 15 months older than Tony, never really had time to be a baby. She was obliged to grow up quickly, which was relatively easy for her as she had been born with a very independent spirit (SnR (Moon) in Aquarius with Ovl in Sagittarius).

A sun-sign Cancerian, from the start Janet showed the world a tough exterior, although masking it somewhat by polite diplomacy (Virgo ChR; Taurus Asc). She was independently minded with a need to 'do her own thing', and learned to walk earlier than most, at around ten months, well before the birth of her brother. This independent streak was to prove both a blessing and a curse as the years passed.

Tony, on the other hand, was a home-loving boy (IC Taurus). His birthday came only one day after his mother's and gave him Sun in Virgo very close to hers. He, however, had Scorpio Ovl as opposed to his mother, Margaret's Pisces – both in water signs, but the son's far stronger and more dominant than the mother's. He also had a practical Capricorn Asc with Scorpio again on the MC.

There was a quiet power and a magnetic force about this very loving and caring boy (strong Scorpio Ovls). His Moon/DecR lay at 06° 45′ Gemini – quite close to his grandfather's IC 02° 06′. His own Asc 16° 50′ Capricorn lay near his grandfather's Asc at 22° 19′ and his ChR at 24° 50′ Cancer was close to his grandmother's Asc. His SnR (Mercury) lay near to his father's Libran Sun and he had the warm fire sign of Leo as his Mn Ovl. His IC Ovl also lay in this sign, again close to his grandfather's, while another fire sign, independent Sagittarius, was SnR/MnR Ovl – like his sister. He had Aquarius strongly placed as MC Ovl and ICR Ovl (close to his sister's Mn). Therefore, the independent side that has been so dominant in her was also in his make-up, but it made itself felt in a more subtle way (the strong Scorpio content probably accounting for this). How he would have developed we can but conjecture, for tragically at only 12 years of age he died.

Janet became the soul focus of her parents' world. Her father, particularly, who never got over the loss of his son, doted upon his remaining child. He was proud of her academic achievements but devastated when she announced that she was going abroad to teach. She had not long begun her travels when her broken-hearted father died from a sudden heart attack, leaving her mother totally alone.

Although since that time Janet has spent spasmodic periods in England – during one of which she married her Mexican fiancé – she has never really settled anywhere permanently. She lived for a few years in Mexico, where her son was born, then moved to France – during which time her daughter was born. England was the next destination and finally the whole family returned to Mexico. The final move? I wonder!

The Fifth Grandchild

The last of the five cousins is Richard (Alice's son; Barbara's brother). His Sun, like his cousin Janet's, is in Cancer. His astrological mix is similar to his Aunt Ciss's, but his early home life did not have the stability of hers. He, like his sister, was born into a home where mother and father were almost permanently at odds. His supersensitive blend of signs made him more vulnerable than his sister to the atmosphere of animosity and moodiness in which he had to develop. Physically he was not a well child and suffered terribly from asthma (Cancer Sn and ChR, Pisces SnR/MCR). Things got even worse for the little boy when his sister left home to go to university. At about the same time his cousin, Tony, whom he loved and admired as both friend and companion, suddenly died, and his mother's mental state began to deteriorate.

Throughout all the heartache and difficulties, his love for his parents (particularly for his mother) remained staunch and devoted. Even so, like his sister before him, he felt the need to get away and find his own niche in the world (Jupiter strong in its own sign – incidentally there is 12 years difference in their ages but both of them have Jupiter in this sign on almost the same degree!). Since that period he has changed directions several times and seems to be eternally searching for something – the emotional security lacking in his early childhood perhaps? The Virgo Ovl of his Moon (his SnR/MCR) combining with the tendency of Cancer (the strongest sign in his chart) to hide its feelings, makes him very much a loner, at least as far as his family is concerned.

Before moving on to the next generation, let us take a closer look at some of the hereditary connections found between grandparents and grandchildren.

We have already seen the strong Taurus content passed down from Mary and Jim to their children and now we see how the trend continues to a third generation.

Rosemary (Sue's daughter)
Sn 24° 33′; SnR (Venus) Ovl 25° 06′
Barbara (Alice's daughter)
Dec 18° 08′, Mn Ovl 25° 38′
Janet (Margaret's daughter)
Asc 21° 33′; IC Ovl 29° 16′; Jupiter Ovl 20° 30′
Tony (Margaret's son)
IC 24° 51′
Richard (Alice's son)
DecR 16° 34′

The continuance of the Taurus content to yet another generation is reinforced by the fact that the three girls married men with this sign of the zodiac prominent in their charts. Of the two boys, one died at a very early age and the other has remained single to date.

Rosemary's husband: Mercury 24° 20′ (Mercury is the most important planet in her chart), Sun 10° 02′; DecR Ovl 08° 07′ and ICR Uranus (her ChR) 09° 37′ (only 14′ separation from her grandfather's Moon).

Barbara's husband: Sn 24° 30′; ChR/SnR (Venus) Ovl 25° 08′ (Venus is her DecR), Asc 10° 39′, MnR (Mercury) 00° 37′ (Mercury is her MCR), Mars 26° 06′ and Uranus Ovl 26° 27′.

Janet's husband: Dec 14° 24′ Sn/MCR Ovl 15° 02′.

We will look further at the apparent fascination of 'start attraction' between couples in a later chapter. For the moment let us scrutinize some other connections.

Gemini:
Mary's Mercury (SnR/ICR) is found in the exact same position as Rosemary's Uranus (ChR) at 00° 03′. Jim's IC 02° 06′ is also very close not only to Rosemary's ChR 00° 03′ and her Moon, 03° 32′, but also Janet's Mn Ovl at 01° 51′.

Cancer:
Mary's Asc 28° 58′ and Jim's Dec 22° 19′, close to Rosemary's IC Ovl 27° 08′; Barbara's Sn (IC OvlR) 27° 01′, Janet's Sn 23° 53′; MnR 23° 24′ and Richard's MC 28° 38′; Mn OvR 26° 43′; ChR 26° 52′. Jim's Mn Ovl (Mn is his DecR/MnOvR) 17° 32′

is close to Rosemary's Mn Ovl 17° 44′ (Mn is her Sn and Mn OvlR and IC OvlR); MCOvlR Ovl 15° 07′; ChR Ovl 14° 15′ and Janet's IC 20° 49′; Tony's Dec 16° 50′ and Richard's Sn 21° 06′. Janet's Mn OvlR 12° 03′ and ChR/IC OvlR Ovl 12° 38′ are not too far away; Jim's MCR (Jupiter) 01° 19′ is close to Barbara's MCR Ovl 03° 31′ and Janet's DecR/MC OvlR Ovl 02° 16′, and not too far away from Richard's IC Ovl 07° 39′.

Scorpio:
Jim's Sn, 03° 34′ is close to Janet's MCR 02° 44′, and her brother Tony's MCR 10° 15′ and ICR 17° 15′ are close to Jim's Mars 16° 31′ (Mars is sub-ruler of Scorpio). Mary's MC Ovl 25° 35′ is found close to Janet's Dec 21° 33′ and MC Ovl 29° 16′ and Tony's MC 24° 51′, Sn Ovl 28° 25′.

Capricorn:
Mary's Dec 28° 58′ and MCR Ovl 13° 14′, and Jim's Asc 22° 19′, are found close to Rosemary's MC Ovl 27° 08′ and Janet's MC 20° 49′.

There are many more connections which I will leave you to find for yourselves. However, a couple of very close connections do need a little explanation and do not apparently fall into the dominant formula, but are too close for coincidence.

Grandmother Mary's Jupiter at 11° 54′ Aries and Jupiter Ovl at 12° 56′ Sagittarius are very close to Rosemary's SnR (Venus) at 10° 54′ Aries and exactly the same as her MC, 12° 56′ Sagittarius. Jupiter is not a personal planet in the grandmother's chart but it is the ruler of Rosemary's Sagittarian MC, thus by planetary connections the connection does, in fact, conform.

In the next chapter we look at the astrological inheritance in the fourth and fifth generations.

Chapter 9

Younger Generations and the Final Factor

The fourth generation consists of four girls and two boys; second cousins – or first ones once removed (I'm never really sure!).

The First Great-grandchild

The first child of this generation, Harry A., was born only four years after the birth of the last in the previous one. Harry is Rosemary's son and Sue's grandson. Like his mother before him, he was a quick starter, showing early promise which unfortunately never materialized into anything substantial.

Harry learned to walk and talk at a very early age and was pulling himself to his feet and walking round his cot long before most babies manage to sit up by themselves. By the age of eight months he could walk unaided. His speech too was not only clear and fluent but also exceedingly early in establishing itself. At the astounding age of three he began reading, of his own accord! By the time he started school at four years old, he was a proficient and avid reader (and has remained such to the present day.) But that is where the 'genius' fizzled out . . .

He was born the first grandchild on both sides of the family and was doted upon as such. For five years he was 'king of his own domain', and revelled in it!, Then, not only was his paternal grandfather, Harry W., killed in a traffic accident, but his parents had another child – a daughter. (Only days separated the two events.) The little boy had his nose pushed out of joint or at least he felt as if he did. Suddenly young Harry saw the world in different terms (Scorpio DecR, 15° 32′ – directly from Sue's MC Ovl, 18° 17'). A large chip grew on his shoulder, where it is still firmly established today! He felt that his sister had taken away the affection of his parents. He could not, and still cannot, see that they are capable of loving both children equally.

The trouble was that Harry was born with a deep and devious nature (Sn, Mn, Asc and ruler of them all, Mercury, in that most difficult of signs, Virgo – once more taking its negative form). He also had an obstinate attitude and an abrasive turn of phrase (ICR and DecR Ovl in Taurus; Mn Ovl Aries). He was given every opportunity to do well in life, being sent to a small private school to try to develop his obvious mental abilities. Here he was encouraged to stand on his own feet whilst being taught to work as part of a team. He was urged to join various youthful organizations – all with the aim of equipping him for life.

There was a major problem, however: a clash of personalities and outlook between father and son. This was made particularly difficult because of the obstinate (Taurus) and hot-tempered (Aries) make-up of his father's temperament. It was almost impossible for them to agree on anything and since the father was by far the stronger character, the son felt himself imprisoned by someone else's ideals and principles. In adulthood the animosity towards his father's way of thinking has completely coloured his way of life. Everything his father believes in he automatically abhors!

Yet in spite of this clash, there remains a bond between them that refuses to be broken. Secretly, and despite himself, he admires his father's strength of character and knows that (most of the time) his principles are the right ones. He also realizes that even though his father has always come down on him with a heavy hand, he has done so for the right reasons; because he loved him and wanted him to make the best of himself. Where the problem arose is that in the early years the child was not allowed to develop his own personality and outlook on life. Therefore, in adulthood he chooses the direct opposite of that which was previously imposed upon him.

The Second Great-grandchild

The next child of this generation is Harry's sister, Helen. Her astrological mix – despite having an Aries content (Sn Ovl 14° 16') – is far less abrasive than her brother's. She is a Libran sun sign and has this sign too on the Asc. Libra may have its faults but at least they are masked by a gentle and diplomatic exterior.

Helen started life at a much slower pace than her brother. She was a steady, careful and rather serious little girl – the strong Capricorn in her make-up (IC 12° 39'; MC Ovl 03° 15'; Mn/MCR 08° 43' inherited both from her father (Mn 17° 37'; MC Ovl 09° 34') and her maternal grandmother, Sue's Dec 04° 22' MnR/MCR 20° 02' and DecR Ovl 04° 50' which in turn came from her mother, Mary's Mn/ChR 26° 41'; MCR Ovl 13° 14' and Dec 28° 58', and her father, Jim's Asc (22° 19'; Sn Ovl (11° 15') and ICR Ovl (01° 19'). Helen was born ambitious (Capricorn Moon), and although her raw material may not have been potentially as brilliant as her brother's, she took what she had and used it well.

With a strong Libra content in her make-up, she fell in love at the very early age of 15. However, the steady earth influence (Capricorn and Taurus) gave her the common sense not to rush into anything prematurely. She was married just before her 21st birthday to the same boy she had been in love with from the start. Again this steadying influence has stopped her from having a family straight away. She (and her Capricorn sun-sign husband) are determined to have career and home on a good footing before embarking on parenthood, despite both of them longing for a family. One can but wonder what such a practical combination will bring forth in the next generation. I have the sneaking feeling that the irresponsible element may surface once again.

The Third and Fourth Great-grandchildren

Great-grandchildren three and four are Barbara's daughters, Jenny and Elizabeth. As yet they are only teenagers, therefore a full analysis of them would be a bit premature. I will give simply a brief description of them and how I would conjecture they might develop according to their astrological make-up. Then we will look at their inherited astrological placings.

Jenny has grown from a quite chubby youngster into a tall willowy elegant young woman. She has charm (Libra) and charisma (Leo) and the ability to communicate (strong Mercury, her Virgo Sun's ruler). At first glance you would assume that she is a very clever girl – she is certainly diligent, but a closer examination reveals a likely problem in the education field.

I have noted before that when Saturn lies between the Sun and Mercury in a chart (particularly when Mercury is of personal importance – as in this case), it signifies some kind of learning or communicative difficulty. Sometimes it can manifest as a stutter, or it can be indicative of the disability known as dyslexia. We have already found one case of this in the family – in Rosemary. It surfaces once again here.

In this more enlightened age I am sure that any difficulties will be overcome. Jenny has already achieved much despite it and will I am sure continue to do so. Her Leo Asc gives her the necessary need to come out on top! She does have a strong Virgo content in her chart and, as we have seen before, this can be troublesome. However, in her case it takes its positive form which, although not easy to handle, is at least less destructive.

Her sister, Elizabeth, may pose slightly more of a problem. On the face of it she is better placed astrologically to succeed. She is extremely bright and has a natural determination and ambition not only to succeed but also to gain financially from her endeavours. However, she also has a strong stubborn streak and a lazy side to her make-up. (Taurus is exceedingly strongly placed in her chart which could upset the apple cart.)

Elizabeth has inherited her grandmother Alice's Scorpio Moon, which is always a difficult placing to deal with – the emotions run still, deep and silent but are also volatile and vulnerable. She is, however, better placed than Alice was to deal with the abundance of emotional tides. She has a compensating Taurean sun (the signs are each other's polarity, thus should give the necessary balance), whereas her grandmother had to cope with an erratic Aquarian Sun that vied with and irritated her Scorpio Moon! But there is a safety valve present, for Elizabeth has Mars in its own sign of Aries (like her Great-Aunt Kit and like her father's Mars Ovl) and in her case this is a saving grace. Mars in Aries can't help but let off steam and this will help diffuse the build-up of pent-up emotions generated by the Scorpio Moon. Elizabeth should be OK!

Jenny has Leo 13° 55' on the Ascendant, which makes her Virgo Sun (21° 23') her Chart Ruler. This doubly important placing (lies close to her father's Moon position (his ICR) at 17° 14' and his MCR Ovl at 15° 00' Leo). There is also a maternal connection: her maternal grandmother Alice's MCR on 24° 13' Virgo, which in turn was inherited from her mother Mary (Jenny's great-grandmother), who had IC 27° 33' Virgo and ChR Ovl 27° 43' Virgo.

The Ascendant itself connects to her mother Barbara's MnR 17° 19' Leo, which in turn came from her grandfather Jim's IC Ovl 09° 47', and to her paternal grandmother's Sun (SnR/MnR) on 09° 48' Leo and Moon (MCR) 15° 44' Leo.

Jenny's Sn Ovl at 07° 58' Taurus lies close to her sister Elizabeth's Mn Ovl 06° 46' Taurus (by sign 14° 51' Scorpio). These connect firstly with their father's Asc/Dec 10° 39' Taurus/Scorpio, and MnR 00° 37' Taurus, and to their mother's Asc 18° 08' Scorpio. There is also a connection to their great-grandfather Jim, who had Moon 09° 51' Taurus.

You see how the pattern follows through.

The Fifth and Sixth Great-grandchildren

Great-grandchildren five and six are Janet's children. They were both born by Caesarean section, which often throws out the hereditary patterns. Nevertheless, some connections can still be found. They are both still young children, so once again we can only anticipate what may develop.

Johnny is a sensitive boy (Pisces Sun/Scorpio Asc) who has had much disruption and upheaval in his short life. What he needs most of all is a settled, stable environment in which to develop. Now that the family has returned to his native Mexico, perhaps he will get it and begin to achieve the potential of his birthright.

I have a feeling that the religious vocational callings of the first and second generations might just come to the fore again in him.

There is certainly the potential for them to emerge and the fact that he is now growing up in a Catholic country amid a Catholic family makes it appear even more likely.

His sister, Katy, is another matter. She, I feel sure, will develop her mother's itchy feet and take off to do her own thing, probably at an early age. (I wonder how Janet, the Cancerian mum will cope with the trend from this side of the fence!) I cannot see someone of Katy's astrological make-up accepting the second-class citizenship that women still have to endure in Mexico, for already she has a strong personality and a mind of her own. She is adaptive by nature and is a true survivor. I have no real worries on her behalf.

Johnny's Mn Ovl at 04° 36′ Gemini connects to his mother Janet's Sn Ovl (02° 36′ Gemini) and her MnR Ovl (01° 51′ Gemini). The Moon is Janet's SnR. This can be traced back to Johnny's great-grandmother and grandfather – Mary's SnR/ICR at 00° 03′ Gemini and Jim's IC 02° 06′ Gemini.

Katy's SnR/MnR on 29° 34′ Taurus connects to her mother's Asc 21° 33′ Taurus and IC Ovl 29° 16′ Taurus, which in turn goes back to Jim's SnR 29° 36′ Taurus (very close!) and his ChR/SnOvR 24° 11′ Taurus, also to Mary's IC Ovl 25° 35′ Taurus.

The First Great-great Grandson

Finally, we come to the fifth generation. Richard A. is the great-great grandson of our first generation couple, Mary and Jim. He is still only a very small child but some of the connections spanning the full five generations and a century are very close.

Richard is an extremely modern little boy, brought up in a world very different to that of his predecessors. For a start he is being brought up mainly without the influence of his father, within the confines of a one-parent family. He is wilful and quick-tempered (Leo Moon with an Aries overlay and strong Sagittarius content). However, he is also sensitive and very

loving when he wants to be (Cancer Asc). The dreaded
Scorpio/Aquarius mix occurs once more in this little boy, not
quite to the extremes found before, but nevertheless, inner
tensions could erupt into problems both for himself and those
close to him as he develops. The more positive side of his
nature needs to be encouraged in order for these pitfalls to be
avoided. We can but hope, watch and pray.

Richard's IC Ovl on 03° 30′ Gemini relates directly to his
paternal grandmother, Rosemary, who has Mn 03° 32′ and her
ChR 00° 03′ Gemini. These in turn relate back to her maternal
grandfather, Jim's IC 02° 06′ Gemini and her maternal
grandmother, Mary's SnR/ICR 00° 03′ Gemini.

Richard's Mn Ovl on 04° 50′ Aries relates to his father, Harry
A.'s Mn Ovl at 00° 09′ Aries and his paternal grandfather,
Harry S.'s MnR 00° 40′ Aries, which in turn came from his
father, Harry W.'s Mercury 03° 46′ Aries – whether this planet
was a personal placing or not, we do not know as no birth
time is available for him. Rosemary has SnR on 10° 54′ Aries
(the Sun is Richard's Moon Ruler) which in turn came from
her mother, Sue's DecR 09° 12′ Aries (crossing the hereditary
formula). Rosemary's own paternal grandmother, Sarah, had
SnR (Venus) on 05° 00′ Aries.

Richard's Moon (his ChR) lies on 01° 03′ Leo, which relates
directly to Rosemary's MnR/ICR Ovl 00° 30′ Leo directly
from her grandfather Jim's ChR/SnOvR Ovl 01° 52′ Leo and
Harry S.'s MC at 05° 00′ Leo (again crossing the hereditary
formula).

His Sn at 05° 23′ Aquarius also crosses the formula to connect
with his paternal grandfather, Harry S.'s IC on 05° 09′
Aquarius, but it follows the formula on Rosemary's side, her
father, Gerard, having MCR 11° 31′ Aquarius and her
maternal grandmother, Mary, having 07° 51′ Aquarius as her
Sn Ovl and 01° 05′ Aquarius as her SnR/ICR Ovl, and her
maternal grandfather, Jim, having 09° 47′ as MC Ovl.

Richard has 29° 43′ Virgo/Pisces as his MC/IC axis – which
comes directly from his father, Harry A.'s Asc/Dec 28° 28′
Virgo/Pisces. His father also has Mn 28° 37′ Virgo, which in
turn comes from his father, Harry S.'s ChR/SnR Ovl on 25°
00′ Virgo, going back to his mother, Maud's MCR 27° 48′

Virgo. There is also a connection through Rosemary's side. Mary, Richard's great-great grandmother, had Mn Ovl on 27° 43' Virgo and MC/IC 27° 33' Pisces/Virgo.

Richard's Asc/Dec 28° 13' Cancer/Capricorn lies very close to Mary's Asc/Dec on 28° 58' Cancer/Capricorn, with its subsequent hereditary connections through the generations.

Harmonic Aspect Connections – The Final Hereditary Factor

The final category – that of harmonic aspect connections – continues the fascinating interchange, following the same pattern and formula as the personal planets, signs and overlays above. However, with this category I have only compared the charts of parents and children, simply because of the number of degrees involved. The harmonics I looked at were the first harmonic; the second; the third; the fourth; the sixth and both the twelfth (30° and 150°). I used these particular harmonics as they are the most easily detected when looking at a chart. The orbs used were to a maximum of under 2° – most were found to be much closer to within degree minutes rather than whole degrees.

I do not doubt that there are a great many more interconnections to be found, using the smaller harmonics – some of them very probably significant and of great importance – but for the purpose of this book and as a starting-off point for further investigation, I will deal only with the above harmonics.

The results achieved were rather surprising. The close connection and dominance of the first harmonic (the Conjunction) was as expected – there were a great many of them. But it turned out that this was not the most dominant harmonic! The results were:

1 12th harmonic (the Semisextile)
2 1st harmonic (the Conjunction)
3 12th harmonic (the Quincunx)
4 6th harmonic (the Sextile)
5 2nd harmonic (the Opposition)
6 3rd harmonic (the Trine)
7 4th harmonic (the Square)

What took me by surprise was the frequency of the twelfth harmonic. I suppose it shouldn't have done, when you think about it logically. What does the twelfth harmonic indicate? Strain, tension and incompatibility. The other eight signs all have something in common with each other; only at the 30° or the 150° distance do they have nothing at all. When you look at a sign of the zodiac, its neighbouring signs and the neighbouring signs of its polarity are totally at odds with it. There is, in other words, incomprehension between them.

The dominance, therefore, of this harmonic is a perfect explanation for the generation gap! When parents and or grandparents exclaim with exasperation, 'I just don't understand the younger generation!' – that is absolutely true (and vice versa), they don't; they can't; the dominance of the twelfth harmonic aspects between them means that they view life from totally different perspectives!

I will not fill up the pages of this book with rows and rows of figures to corroborate my findings, but I will give a few examples. I do suggest, however, that you take a look at the degree connections in the charts of your own family. I am sure you will find it, as I did, a fascinating and rewarding exercise.

A Final Summing Up of 'Peel's Law' of Astrological Heredity

The hereditary connections come in three ways by:

1 Sign and overlay placements
2 Personal planet involvement
3 Aspect harmonic connections

They chiefly follow a dominant two-group formula:

Asc/Mn/IC and MC/Sn/Dec

N.B. When examining a planet or point, the actual sign placing, its overlay placing and the placings of the sign and overlay rulers must be taken into account.

Within the dominant formula groups the following are dominant.

First generation:
Direct inheritance from the father (Asc to Asc; Sn to Sn etc.).
Indirect inheritance from the mother (Asc to Mn; Sn to MC
etc. interchanges). Also, between the first and second generations, signs and overlays tend to swap, i.e parents' overlays
become children's signs and vice versa.

Second generation:
Either direct or indirect inheritance but Mn to IC and IC to
Asc interchanges and Sn to Dec and Dec to MC interchanges
more frequent. Between the first and third generations, signs
and overlays tend to remain the same, i.e grandparents' signs
or overlays remain signs or overlays in grandchildren.

Note: These are not hard and fast rules, but they are dominant
features within the dominant formula. As in genetics, recessive
features (those not conforming to the above) can and do apply,
but not with the same frequency.
   Let us now look at each of the three categories, using the MC
of our fourth generation second child, Helen, as our example:

1 Sign and overlay placings

Sign 12° 39′ Cancer:	Mother's DecR (Sn) Ovl 08° 45′ Cancer
	Mat. G'Mother's Sn OvlR 13° 53′ Cancer
	Mat. G'G'Father's Mn/DecR/ MnOvR 17° 32′ Cancer
Overlay 3° 15′ Capricorn:	Mat. G'Mother's Dec 04° 22′ Capricorn
	Mat. G'Mother's DecR Ovl 04° 50′ Capricorn
	Mat. G'Father's Dec 02° 10′ Capricorn
MCR 08° 43′ Capricorn:	Father's MC Ovl 09° 34′ Capricorn
	Mat. G'Mother's Dec 04° 22′ Capricorn
	Mat. G'Mother's DecR Ovl 04° 50′ Capricorn
	Mat. G'G'Mother's MCR Ovl 13° 14′ Capricorn
	Mat. G'G'Father's Sn/IC OvR 11° 15′ Capricorn

MCR Overlay 29° 19' Gemini:	Mother's MCR 24° 23' Gemini
	Mat. G'Father's SnR 28° 07' Gemini
	Mat. G'Father's DecR 20° 12' Gemini
	Pat. G'Mother's Dec 28° 01' Gemini
MCOvR 06° 24' Taurus:	Father's MCR (Sn) 10° 02' Taurus
	Father's DecR Ovl 08° 07' Taurus
	Father's ICR 09° 37' Taurus
	Mat. G'G' Father's Mn 09° 51' Taurus
MCOvR Ovl 27° 00' Libra:	Pat. G'Mother's MC 24° 02' Libra
	Father's Asc 25° 35' Libra
	Mat. G'G'Father's ICR 23° 38' Libra

2 Personal planets

MC's personal planets = Moon; Mercury, Saturn and Jupiter

Moon:	Father's Mn Ovl 22° 02' Gemini
	Mother's Mn Ovl 17° 44' Cancer
	Mat. G'Father's Mn Ovl 16° 41' Gemini
Mercury:	Mother's Mer 16° 18' Gemini
	Father's Mer Ovl 25° 45' Libra
	Mat. G'Father's Mer 28° 07' Gemini
	Mat. G'Mother's Mer 17° 08' Cancer
Saturn:	Mother's Sat Ovl 15° 07' Cancer
	Mat. G'Father's Sat 20° 12' Gemini
	Mat. G'Mother's Sat Ovl 04° 50' Capricorn
Jupiter:	Mother's Jup 24° 23' Gemini
	Mat. G'Mother's Jup Ovl 07° 33' Taurus
	Pat. G'Father's Jup 12° 42' Capricorn
	Mat. G'G'Mother's Jup 25° 00' Libra
	Mat. G'G'Father's Mn Ovl 17° 32' Cancer Mn 09° 51' Taurus Mer 23° 38' Libra

3 Aspect harmonics

MC 12° 39′ Cancer is:

12H Mother's MC 12° 56′ Sagittarius
12H Mat. G'Father's MCR 11° 31′ Aquarius
12H Mat. G'Mother's Jup 11° 55′ Leo
12H Mat. G'G'Mother's Jup Ovl 12° 56′ Sagittarius
2H Mat. G'G'Mother's MCR Ovl 13° 14′ Capricorn
2H Pat. G'Father's Jup 12° 42′ Capricorn
2H Mat. G'G'Father's Sn Ovl 11° 15′ Capricorn
4H Mat. G'Mother's SnR (Mer) Ovl 12° 46′ Aries
4H Mat. G'G'Mother's Jup 11° 54′ Aries
6H Mat. G'G' Mother's MCR 12° 42′ Taurus

MC Ovl 03° 15′ Capricorn is:

12H Mother's Mn 03° 32′ Gemini
12H Father's MC 05° 09′ Leo
12H Father's IC 05° 09′ Aquarius
12H Father's DecR 03° 42′ Sagittarius
12H Mat. G'G'Father's MC 02° 06′ Sagittarius
12H Mat. G'G'Father's IC 02° 06′ Gemini
4H Pat. G'Father's Mer 03° 46′ Aries
1H Mat. G'Father's Asc 02° 10′ Cancer
1H Mat. G'Mother's Asc 04° 22′ Cancer
6H Mat. G'G'Father's Sn 03° 34′ Scorpio
1H Mat. G'G'Father's MCR 01° 19′ Cancer

MCR 08° 43′ Capricorn is: 12H Mother's MCR Ovl 08° 35′ Leo

 12H Mat. G'G'Mother's Sn Ovl 07° 51′ Aquarius

 12H Mat. G'G'Father's SnR Ovl 07° 17′ Leo

 1H Father's MC Ovl 09° 34′ Capricorn

 3H Father's DecR Ovl 08° 07′ Taurus

 2H Mother's DecR Ovl 08° 45′ Cancer

 6H Mat. G'Father's Sn Ovl 08° 38′ Pisces

 6H Mat. G'Father's MCR Ovl 09° 21′ Scorpio

 4H Mat. G'Mother's DecR 09° 12′ Aries

 3H Mat. G'G'Father's Mn 09° 51′ Taurus

 3H Mat. G'G'Father's MCR 09° 00′ Virgo

 12H Mat. G'G'Father's MC Ovl 09° 47′ Aquarius

 12H Mat. G'G'Father's IC Ovl 09° 47′ Leo

MCR Ovl 29° 19′ Gemini is: 12H Mother's MC Ovl 27° 08′ Capricorn

 12H Mother's IC Ovl 27° 08′ Cancer

 12H Pat. G'Mother's Dec 28° 01′ Gemini

 12H Pat. G'Mother's Asc 28° 01′ Sagittarius

 12H Mat. G'G'Mother's Dec 28° 58′ Capricorn

 12H Mat. G'G'Mother's Asc 28° 58′ Cancer

 12H Mat. G'G'Father's Snr 29° 36′ Taurus

2H Mat. G'G' Father's MnR Ovl
28° 55' Sagittarius

1H Mat. G'Father's SnR 28° 07'
Gemini

6H Pat. G'Mother's Mn 28° 14'
Aries

4H Pat. G'Mother's MCR 27°
48' Virgo

2H Pat. G'Mother's MCR Ovl
29° 47' Sagittarius

3H Mat. G'G'Mother's MC 27°
33' Pisces

6H Mat. G'G'Mother's IC 27°
33' Virgo

6H Mat. G'G'Mother's Mn
(ChR) Ovl 27° 43' Virgo

12H Mat. G'G'Father's SnR 29° 36'
Taurus

12H Mat. G'G'Father's MC OvlR
29° 19' Scorpio

MCOvR 06° 24' Taurus is:

12H Mat. G'Father's Venus Ovl 06°
15' Aries

12H Mat. G'G'Mother's Sn 06° 49'
Gemini

12H Mat. G'G'Mother's SnR 05°
00' Aries (approx.)

6H Mat. G'G'Father's Sn 07° 00'
Leo (approx.)

1H Mat. G'G'Mother's Sn 05° 00'
Taurus (approx.)

4H Mat. G'G'Mother's Sn Ovl 07°
51' Aquarius

4H Mother's MCR Ovl 08° 35'
Leo

4H Father's MC 05° 09' Leo

4H Father's IC 05° 09' Aquarius

MCOvR Ovl 27° 00' Libra is:

12H Pat. G'Mother's MCR 27° 48'
Virgo

12H Pat. G'Father's Saturn 28° 27'
Taurus

12H Mat. G'G'Mother's MC 27°
33' Pisces
12H Mat. G'G'Mother's IC 27° 33'
Virgo
4H Mat. G'G'Mother's Dec 28° 58'
Capricorn
4H Mat. G'G'Mother's Asc 28° 58'
Cancer
4H Mother's MC Ovl 27° 08'
Capricorn
4H Mother's IC Ovl 27° 08'
Cancer
4H Mat. G'G'Mother's Mn 26°
41' Capricorn
4H Mat. G'G'Mother's Mn Ovl
27° 43' Virgo
6H Mat. G'G'Father's Venus Ovl
(MnR) 28° 55' Sagittarius

This, then, is how astrological heredity works. If you wish to examine it for yourself, the data at the back of this work will give you all the necessary information. I also hope that you will experiment with your own family, for I am sure you will find it a worthwhile and enjoyable experience.

In the next chapter we will examine a phenomena I call 'Star Attraction'. I will also look towards the future as the world enters a new astrological age as, at long last, Aquarius dawns!

Chapter 10

'Star Attraction'

During the years of research for a hereditary connection I accumulated a great deal of family data. From this I noticed that time and time again there seemed to be a physical attraction between people of similar astrological backgrounds. The more I studied this, the more sure I became that this was not just a haphazard occurrence but a part of our astrological make-up. It seems that we have a subconscious attraction to someone who is likely to reinforce our own astrological inheritance in the next generation! Thus, with the intermingling of other families through generation upon generation, the same family patterns are preserved.

Let us take a look at this phenomena through the family data we have already examined in the hereditary connection, beginning once again with the first generation.

Mary and Jim have a lot of close connections in their charts. The outstanding ones are:

Mary:	SnR/ICR	00° 03' Gemini
	Sn	06° 49' Gemini
Jim:	ChR Ovl	01° 28' Gemini
	IC	02° 06' Gemini
also	Jim's Asc	22° 41' Capricorn
	Mary's Moon	26° 41'
	and Dec	28° 58' Capricorn
Mary:	Venus (his MnR)	24° 19' Taurus
	IC Ovl	25° 35' Taurus
Jim:	ChR/SnOR (her MnR)	24° 11' Taurus
	Mn Ovl	23° 32' Taurus
Mary:	Jupiter Ovl (his MCR)	12° 56' Sagittarius
Jim:	MnR (Venus)	15° 14' Sagittarius

The astrological connections between them are quite clear.

The second generation has some gaps in the available data. Most of the details of the husbands and wives (with the exception of Sue's husband) are without birth times, nor do we have any data for their parents. Even in Gerard's case, his data cannot be taken as exact since his chart was rectified from an approximate time stated. The data for his parents are available, but once again without times. Therefore, there is not enough accurate data to look at the 'star attraction' features for this generation.

However, it is worth noting that the four girls who married all chose men with an air sun sign. Sue's husband had sun at 10° 48' Gemini (quite close to her mother's at 06° 49'; Alice's husband also had sun within this area, at 10° approximately; Margaret's husband had sun at 13° Libra and Kit's husband had an Aquarian Sun (degree not known).

In the third generation, once again, there are gaps in the astrological data, but there are enough available for us to see how the trend continues.

1 Rosemary and Harry S.

Her: Sun 24° 33' Taurus (the Sun is his MCR)

Him: Mercury 24° 20' Taurus (Mercury is her MnR/ICR)

Her:	MnR/ICR (Mercury)	16° 18' Gemini
	MCR (Jupiter)	24° 23' Gemini
Him:	Mn Ovl	22° 02' Gemini

Her:	MC Ovl	27° 08' Capricorn
Him:	Jupiter	27° 37' Capricorn
	(her MCR)	

We can also look at some of the connections between them and their in-laws.

Rosemary's father, Gerard:		Harry S:	
Mn (ChR) Ovl	16° 41' Gemini	Mn Ovl	22° 02' Gemini
Mn (ChR)	18° 51' Virgo	ChR/SnR Ovl	25° 00' Virgo

Rosemary's mother, Sue: Harry S:

MCR/MnR Ovl 15° 40' Libra   ICR Ovl   14° 02' Libra
(Uranus is Sue's MCR/MnR)   (Uranus is his ICR)

Harry S.'s mother, Maud: Rosemary:

Sn/SnR   21° 41' Leo   Dec   15° 48' Leo
MC Ovl   26° 01' Capricorn   MC Ovl   27° 08' Capricorn
Dec   28° 01' Gemini   MCR   24° 23' Gemini

No birth time is available for his father.

2 Barbara and Andrew

Barbara: Mn Ovl   25° 38' Taurus (his ICR)

Andrew: Sn   24° 30' Taurus
           ChR/SnR Ovl (Mercury)   25° 08' Taurus

Barbara: MCR Ovl (Mercury)   03° 31' Cancer (his MnR)

Andrew: ChR/SnR (Venus)   05° 47' Cancer (his DecR)

Once again there are also in-law connections.

Barbara's mother, Alice: Andrew:

IC   06° 39' Cancer   ChR/SnR   05° 47' Cancer
Asc   19° 00' Aries   Mars Ovl   15° 27' Aries
                                       (Mars is Alice's ChR)
MCR (Saturn) 24° 13' Virgo   MCR (Saturn) 25° 39' Virgo

Barbara's father, John D: Andrew:

Sn   10° 00' Gemini   IC Ovl   06° 25' Gemini
SnR (Mercury) 03° 00' Cancer   ChR/SnR   05° 47' Cancer

(The placings for John D. are to the nearest degree – no birth time is
known.)

Andrews's mother, Joan: Barbara:

 Asc   07° 24' Libra   SnR/ICR   12° 22' Libra
SnR/MnR   09° 48' Leo   ChR   13° 06' Leo
MCR   15° 44' Leo   MnR   17° 19' Leo
DecR Ovl   27° 06' Leo   IC Ovl   21° 02' Leo
Sn Ovl   02° 24' Pisces   Sn   15° 09' Pisces
MCR (Mn) Ovl 08° 20' Pisces   IC   09° 10' Pisces

DecR	04° 30′ Pisces		
IC	09° 39′ Capricorn	Mn	13° 46′ Capricorn
MC	09° 39′ Cancer	MCR Ovl	03° 31′ Cancer
ChR Ovl	25° 34′ Sagittarius	MnR Ovl	29° 11′ Sagittarius
		ChR Ovl	24° 58′ Sagittarius

Andrew's father, John N:		Barbara:	
Sn	06° 39′ Cancer	MCR Ovl	03° 31′ Cancer
Mn	19° 12′ Capricorn	Mn	13° 46′ Capricorn
MnR	13° 30′ Libra	SnR/ICR	12° 22′ Libra

John N.'s placings are approximate – no birth time is known.

3 Janet and Juan

Her:	ChR	04° 11′ Virgo
His:	ChR	00° 21′ Virgo
Her:	DecR	23° 49′ Leo (Juan's ChR)
His:	MC	15° 32′ Leo
Her:	SnR/ICR Ovl	14° 20′ Sagittarius
His:	SnR	08° 28′ Sagittarius

There are no details for his parents.

Janet's mother, Margaret:		Juan:	
ICR	14° 06′ Aquarius	Mn Ovl	18° 04′ Aquarius
Uranus	08° 22′ Aquarius	IC	15° 32′ Aquarius
(Juan's ICR)		Jupiter Ovl	16° 35′ Aquarius
		(Margaret's ICR)	
ICR Ovl	24° 23′ Leo	Mars Ovl	25° 02′ Leo
		(Margaret's MnR)	

Before we take this 'star attraction' on to the next generation, a closer look at the three husbands proves most informative. Rosemary's husband, Harry S., like Barbara's husband, Andrew, has a Taurean Sun. Janet's husband, Juan's Sun lies in Capricorn, but its overlay is Taurus – coincidence? Perhaps. Harry S. has a Capricorn Moon, Andrew has Capricorn on the MC and, as already stated, Juan has a Capricorn Sun.

What's more, Andrew was born on the same birthday as his wife's cousin, Rosemary, giving them both Sun in the region of 24° to 25° Taurus, almost exactly the same placing as Barbara's Moon overlay and close to Janet's ascendant. Harry

S.'s Moon at 17° 37' Capricorn is quite near to Barbara's Moon at 13° 46' Capricorn and Janet's MC on 20° 49'. Juan's Asc 14° 24' Scorpio is close to Barbara's Asc 18° 08' Scorpio and Janet's Dec on 21° 33' of the same sign. There are many more such 'coincidences'!

Harry S. in build and character is typically Taurean, except for the quickness of his temper (from his strong Aries content). He is solid and dependable, practical and reliable, all traits that Rosemary instinctively needed to bring stability to her life. Although she herself has a Taurean Sun, her own make-up is dominated by the highly-strung Gemini content of her chart.

Andrew also has the same steady Taurean traits, but he takes it one stage further. It is the indolent, laid-back, 'don't trouble trouble till trouble troubles you' side of 'the bull' which dominates him. This is the very thing that Barbara was looking for, to compensate for the lack of emotional stability in her early home life. On top of which, she has inherited some of her mother's erratic temperament and her father's aggressive excitability. She not only meets trouble half way – she goes out and looks for it – sometimes before it is even there! Andrew's casual approach to life counterbalances this perfectly.

Juan is a quiet, cautious, careful man, as you might expect with a Capricorn Sun. He is also ambitious. To all intents and purposes it is Janet who dominates the partnership, but Juan has a Scorpio Asc and in this position Scorpio is a quiet powerhouse with chameleon qualities. Juan is far more dominant and determined than he appears to be to outsiders. Where minor matters are concerned, true his wife rules the roost, but when it really matters, he makes up his mind and she complies. The two most important men in Janet's life both died whilst she was quite young – her brother and her beloved father. She loved both, but idolized her father. Her mother was unable to fill her emotional needs and when her father was suddenly taken from her, she needed someone to fill the fatherly gap. Juan fitted this role perfectly.

Let us now take this fascinating study on to the next generation.

So far, only two of this generation have married. In the case of Harry A. though, he 'partnered' another girl, Wendy, before his marriage. It is she who is the mother of his child. A look at both women gives us some interesting information. First, let's look at his sister, Helen, and her husband, David.

Helen:			*David:*	
ChR/SnR Ovl	20° 08' Pisces		Asc	14° 02' Pisces
			Mn Ovl	09° 33' Pisces
Uranus Ovl	27° 56' Pisces		SnR	24° 53' Pisces
(David's MnR)				
MC Ovl	03° 15' Capricorn		MC	23° 48' Sagittarius
IC Ovl	03° 15' Cancer		IC	23° 48' Gemini
Mn Ovl	29° 19' Gemini			
DecR	16° 57' Capricorn		Sn	22° 32' Capricorn
Mn/MCR	08° 43' Capricorn		DecR/ICR	19° 37' Capricorn
			MC Ovl	09° 46' Capricorn
ChR/SnR	29° 32' Virgo		MnR	24° 19' Virgo
Sn Ovl	14° 16' Aries		SnR Ovl	10° 51' Aries
Uranus	07° 20' Libra		MnR Ovl	10° 17' Libra
(his MnR)				

Helen's father, Harry S:		David:	
MC	05° 09' Leo	MCR	00° 22' Leo
IC	05° 09' Aquarius	DecR/ICR Ovl	05° 35' Aquarius
		Venus	08° 17' Aquarius
		(Harry S.'s ChR/SnR)	
Mn	17° 37' Capricorn	DecR/ICR	19° 37' Capricorn
MC Ovl	09° 34' Capricorn	MC Ovl	09° 46' Capricorn
IC Ovl	09° 34' Cancer	IC Ovl	09° 46' Cancer
ICR Ovl	14° 02' Libra	MnR Ovl	10° 17' Libra
		Mars	19° 40' Libra
		(Harry S.'s DecR)	
ChR/SnR Ovl	25° 00' Virgo	MnR	24° 19' Virgo

Helen's mother, Rosemary:		David:	
MnR/ICR Ovl	00° 03' Leo	MCR	00° 22' Leo
MC Ovl	27° 08' Capricorn	Sn	22° 32' Capricorn
Dec	15° 48' Leo	MCR Ovl	16° 20' Leo
SnR	10° 54' Aries	SnR Ovl	10° 51' Aries

David's mother, Doreen:		Helen:	
ChR/SnR (Venus)	12° 08' Aries		09° 24'
		Dec	14° 10' Aries
		(Venus is Helen's ChR/SnR)	
Dec	04° 25' Aries	Sn Ovl	14° 16' Aries
DecR Ovl	19° 51' Capricorn	MCR/Mn	08° 43' Capricorn
MC Ovl	04° 46' Capricorn	IC	12° 39' Capricorn
Asc	04° 25' Libra		
SnR/ChR Ovl	07° 43' Libra	Mercury	05° 57' Libra
		(Doreen's MnR)	
MnR	12° 10' Taurus	MnR/ICR	06° 24' Taurus
Sn	12° 07' Taurus		
ICR	24° 16' Gemini	MCR/Mn Ovl	29° 19' Gemini
MC	07° 11' Cancer	DecR Ovl	07° 33' Cancer
IC Ovl	04° 46' Cancer		

David's father, Wilf:		Helen:	
Sn	22° 36' Capricorn	DecR	16° 57' Capricorn
DecR	29° 06' Sagittarius	MC Ovl	03° 15' Capricorn
ICR	25° 26' Virgo	ChR/SnR	29° 32' Virgo

Now let's take a look at her brother's connections to both his wife, Karen's placings and his ex-fiancé, Wendy's, (although no birth time is available for her). Harry A.'s Dec is 28° 28' Pisces; he also has Sn Ovl at 16° 13' Pisces and SnR/MnR/MCR/ChR (Mercury) Ovl 07° 15' Pisces. Wendy's Moon is at 21° Pisces (nearest degree at noon on the date of birth – the average movement of the moon on that day was 14° per 24 hours, so this placing can be no more than 7° out). Karen's Moon lies on 20° 32' Pisces – the Moon is her DecR.

Wendy's MnR (Neptune) is at 18° Scorpio approximately. Harry A. has DecR (Neptune) at 15° 32' Scorpio. Wendy has Uranus and Pluto conjunct (1H aspect) on 17° Virgo; Harry A.'s Sn lies at 14° 41' Virgo.

There are probably a great many more connections between these two – and also more similarities to his wife's placings, but we cannot trace them because of the lack of Wendy's birth time – what a pity!

Now let's look at the husband and wife in the same way we have examined the previous partners' placings.

Karen:

Mercury Ovl	04° 01′ Virgo
(his SnR/MnR/ChR/NCR)	
SnR/ICR	21° 45′ Taurus
IC	25° 35′ Taurus
Mercury	21° 45′ Gemini
(his SnR etc.)	
Jupiter Ovl	09° 21′ Scorpio
(his ICR)	

Harry A:

SnR/MnR	
ChR/MCR	04° 43′ Virgo
ICR	26° 01′ Taurus
MC	27° 56′ Gemini
IC Ovl	29° 28′ Gemini
DecR	15° 32′ Scorpio

Karen:

Sn	29° 59′ Taurus
IC	25° 35′ Taurus
SnR/ICR	21° 45′ Taurus
DecR/Mn Ovl	02° 04′ Gemini
Dec	17° 44′ Cancer
SnR/ICR Ovl	04° 01′ Leo

Harry's mother, Rosemary:

Sn	24° 33′ Taurus
SnR Ovl	25° 06′ Taurus
Mn	03° 32′ Gemini
Mn Ovl	17° 44′ Cancer
MCR Ovl	08° 35′ Leo

Karen:

Sn/IC SnR/ICR as above	
MC Ovl	07° 51′ Aquarius
MnR Ovl	07° 20′ Aquarius
ChR	20° 52′ Aries
Asc	17° 44′ Capricorn
MCR Ovl	02° 28′ Sagittarius

Harry's father, Harry S:

Mercury	24° 20′ Taurus
IC	05° 09′ Aquarius
SnR/ChR	20° 35′ Aries
Mn	17° 37′ Capricorn
DecR	03° 42′ Sagittarius

Karen's mother, Linda:

Mn	24° 41′ Pisces
SnR/DecR/	
ICR Ovl	15° 28′ Scorpio
MC	26° 09′ Sagittarius
IC	26° 09′ Gemini
Mn Ovl	05° 51′ Aries
Dec	18° 50′ Virgo

Harry A:

Dec	28° 28′ Pisces
DecR	15° 32′ Scorpio
MC Ovl	29° 28′ Sagittarius
IC	27° 56′ Sagittarius
ICR Ovl	27° 33′ Sagittarius
MC	27° 56′ Gemini
IC Ovl	29° 28′ Gemini
Mn Ovl	00° 09′ Aries
Sn	14° 41′ Virgo

All three 'partners' of this generation, Wendy, Karen and David have the sign of Pisces strongly placed. David has SnR (Saturn) 24° 53′ and Mn Ovl 09° 33′ and Asc 14° 02′, while the two girls, as we have already seen, have Moon at 20° 31′ and 21° (approx.) respectively. Both Harry A. and Helen have this sign strongly as overlays, which comes to them from both sides of the family – although neither of their parents have the sign at all! In three of their four grandparents it features strongly and their maternal great-grandmother (Mary) features it very prominently. It seems that both brother and sister needed to partner someone who would bring this sign back to prominence in future generations. The same theory holds true for the sign of Scorpio.

There does appear to be a very strong connection between the attraction of one person to another through their astrological connections and backgrounds. More research is required to find a definite pattern, but, nevertheless, the evidence is already clear that astrology holds the key to the attraction and repulsion we instinctively feel towards other human beings.

Chapter 11

A Summary

In this final chapter, and in the light of some of the things we have studied, might I suggest that astrology be given a face-lift for the dawning of the new astrological age.

What is the significance of an astrological hereditary link? To my mind it is very important. If our astrological placings can be directly linked to those of our parents and grandparents, then they have not just occurred at random. There must, therefore, be some reason for the recurring patterns. In other words, they give some validity to astrological beliefs – at least as far as birth–chart analysis is concerned.

I have to say that as far as the predictive side of astrology is concerned I, myself, still require a great deal of convincing. This side of astrology has never really interested me. What has given me the most pleasure and kept my interest alive is the ability of the subject to give an insight into the workings of human nature and to offer at least some explanation of the complexities therein. If, by this hereditary link, astrology is proved valid, think of the implications – the uses that birth–chart analysis could be put to. For example, imagine the advantage to parents of knowing a child's character potential *from day one of its life.* What a significant breakthrough that would be in parent/child understanding and relationships. What a boon for mums and dads – think of the pitfalls and the heartaches that could be avoided!

The great Scottish poet, Robbie Burns, once wisely wrote, 'Wad some gift; the giftie gie us: to see oorselves as others see us!'

Astrological analysis gives the ability to do just that, provided one is honest enough to face up to the unpalatable, as well as the palatable, results. I really do believe that astrology can provide a tool for the greater understanding of mankind. That being so, it stands to reason that the sign of Aquarius and its ruler, Uranus, are associated strongly with the subject. At the present time, when signs of the arrival of the age of Aquarius are ever more pronounced, the subject should begin to come into its own. It should be taken out of the category of 'The Unknown', 'The Supernatural' and 'The Fortune Teller' and find its way to a place of real value as a genuine humanitarian aid. Perhaps sometime in the future it will – but not just yet, I think, for at the moment the world is still experiencing the birth pangs of the New Age!

Indications that the Age of Pisces is ending are very evident and have been so for quite some time. The falling of the Berlin Wall; the crumbling of oppressive authoritarian governments, the natural death of Apartheid, all are in keeping with the humanitarian ideals of Aquarius, and its promise of 'people power'.

I find it quite significant that at the dawning of this age the people who were born with Pluto (the planet of power) in the sign of Leo (the polarity of Aquarius) should be the right age to take the reins and lead the people into a new freedom (Aquarius). But before we get too complacent and optimistic, let us remember two things. Firstly, Aquarius and its ruler, Uranus, are erratic by nature and change through either can be difficult and traumatic. The ideals may be truly humanitarian but the methods are often revolutionary and disturbing and the outcome is not necessarily what was originally envisaged. Aquarius agitates against authority – all authority – and demands independence of mind and body. Great in itself – but no sign requires the reins of authority to keep it in line more than wayward, stubborn, eccentric, Aquarius.

Before the discovery of Uranus, astrologers gave the rulership of Aquarius to Saturn. Saturn still sub-rules. We have not had time to look into sub-rulership in this book, but sub-rulers do have some sway over the signs. I think perhaps, we should be very grateful that serious, cautious, Saturn still maintains some hold over Aquarius, as this age comes into its own.

Secondly, at this present time Pluto is still progressing through its own sign of Scorpio. How very apt and significant that at the moment of transformation from one age to another the planet of transformation should be traversing its own sign! We have all felt the enforced upheavals, personally, and on an international scale, of the movement of Pluto through Scorpio, and, although it is now over half way through, we still have some time to go before it passes fully into Sagittarius. This, like Aquarius, is a sign of freedom an independence. Pluto's travels through Scorpio are in keeping with the coming of a New Age. Even in this modern day, before birth comes the period of labour, and if not quite as painful as it used to be, this is still a stressful and exhausting time. We are, I believe, living through the labour pains of the Aquarian Age.

Where does that leave astrology? I would like to believe, at the threshold of a new revival, but one more scientifically based than of old. I do not think that sudden recognition by the scientific world will miraculously occur. Personally, I find miracles and magic very hard to believe in. Both to me are simply something that as yet we cannot comprehend but which will be explained logically in time. (This scepticism may be due to the lack of Pisces in my birth chart. Or perhaps it is my Geminian Mercury requiring logical answers to illogical phenomena.)

Therefore, if astrologers want recognition for themselves and the benefits of astrological analysis for mankind, they have to be willing to work for it. This will entail looking at their subject with objective eyes, holding on tightly to beliefs, but being willing to throw out that which does not work. Astrologers should look at things in new ways; try out new ideas; hold on to what is workable (and *provable*); but let go of what is not!

Aquarius has always been the sign of discoverers and scientists who are willing to try the untried, and thus open new doors for mankind. We, astrologers, must take that approach to our subject. Analyse it, test it, try out new ideas and be flexible enough to move forward. I do not pretend to have the answers – nor even all the questions, but I do believe that we should be looking avidly for both.

My search for a hereditary link has taken me years, but it has been a very worthwhile task. Even if I had not found what I was looking for, the effort would still have been worth expending. On a very personal level, I found a greater understanding of the subject, simultaneously widening my knowledge of the concepts of astrology. As a bonus, I felt that I was able to get to know many people who were no longer alive.

I never knew my paternal grandfather and only have vague memories of my maternal grandparents. My paternal grandmother alone lived long enough to see me reach my teens. My study of their charts revealed to me something of their essence. I felt as if I had known them, maybe in even greater depth than their children had. This, to me, was wonderful. Not only could I feel close to my grandparents, but I could understand their strengths and weaknesses – and could feel both working within myself! Therefore, even if I had never found a hereditary link, I had gained something I would never have possessed, had I not begun the research.

To add to that, my findings have made me rethink my own methods of analysis. For a start I now include houses, but as shadow signs, not as traditional houses. For me, it works. In fact, I have begun to notice something else in relation to the overlays. As we grow older it has always been understood that the power of our birth charts seems to diminish. But what I have noticed, at least as far as the signs are concerned, is that the overlays seem to gain in strength.

What appears to be emerging (but needs more study) is that at birth and for the early years of our lives, the actual sign placings show most strongly. As we approach middle age, the overlays begin to be felt equally powerfully and as we reach old age, the overlays tend to dominate the picture. I do not say that this is always the case, but I think it warrants further investigation.

My hope is that this book has given the reader a greater interest in the fascinating subject of astrology and that perhaps it may help to stimulate further investigation by those with brighter minds and greater material resources than myself.

Astrological Data of the Example Family

Note: The overlays for ascendant and descendent are the same for everyone – 00° 00′ Aries and 00° 00′ Libra – which indicates the basic selfishness (Aries) in all of us and the in-born need to relate to other human beings (Libra) – both necessary for the survival of the species.

The First Generation

MARY: born Greenock, Scotland; 0750 GMT, 27 May 1880

	Rulership	*Sign*	*Overlay*
Ascendant		28° 58′ Cancer	00° 00′ Aries
Descendent		28° 58′ Capricorn	00° 00′ Libra
Midheaven		27° 33′ Pisces	25° 35′ Scorpio
Nadir		27° 33′ Virgo	25° 35′ Taurus
Sun		06° 49′ Gemini	07° 51′ Aquarius
Moon	ChR	26° 41′ Capricorn	27° 43′ Virgo
Mercury	SnR/ICR/ MnOvR	00° 03′ Gemini	01° 05′ Aquarius
Venus	ICOvR	24° 19′ Taurus	25° 21′ Capricorn
Mars		27° 01′ Cancer	28° 03′ Pisces
Jupiter		11° 54′ Aries	12° 56′ Sagittarius
Saturn	MnR/DecR	24° 38′ Aries	25° 40′ Sagittarius
Uranus	Sn OvR	04° 58′ Virgo	06° 00′ Taurus
Neptune	MCR	12° 42′ Taurus	13° 14′ Capricorn
Pluto	MCOvR	27° 01′ Taurus	28° 03′ Capricorn

JIM: born Greenock, Scotland; 1400 GMT, 26 October 1882

	Rulership	Sign	Overlay
Ascendant		22° 19' Capricorn	00° 00' Aries
Descendent		22° 19' Cancer	00° 00' Libra
Midheaven		02° 06' Sagittarius	09° 47' Aquarius
Nadir		02° 06° Gemini	09° 47' Leo
Sun	ICOvR	03° 34' Scorpio	11° 15' Capricorn
Moon	DecR/MnOR	09° 51' Taurus	17° 32' Cancer
Mercury	ICR	23° 38' Libra	01° 19' Capricorn
Venus	MnR	15° 14' Sagittarius	22° 55' Aquarius
Mars		16° 31' Scorpio	24° 12' Capricorn
Jupiter	MCR	01° 19' Cancer	09° 00' Virgo
Saturn	ChR/SnOR	24° 11' Taurus	01° 52' Leo
Uranus	MCOvR	21° 38' Virgo	29° 19' Scorpio
Neptune		17° 47' Taurus	25° 28' Cancer
Pluto	SnR	29° 36' Taurus	07° 17' Leo

The Second Generation

CISS: born Greenock, Scotland; 1220 GMT, 14 March 1907

	Rulership	Sign	Overlay
Ascendant		24° 17' Cancer	00° 00' Aries
Descendent		24° 17' Capricorn	00° 00' Libra
Midheaven		20° 12' Pisces	25° 55' Scorpio
Nadir		20° 12' Virgo	25° 55' Taurus
Sun		26° 24' Pisces	02° 07' Sagittarius
Moon	ChR	26° 24' Pisces	02° 07' Sagittarius
Mercury	ICR	27° 28' Pisces	03° 11' Sagittarius
Venus	ICOvR	08° 38' Aquarius	12° 21' Libra
Mars		20° 46' Sagittarius	26° 29' Leo
Jupiter	SnOvR/MnOvR	01° 27' Cancer	07° 10' Pisces
Saturn	DecR	18° 18' Pisces	24° 01' Scorpio
Uranus		12° 13' Capricorn	17° 56' Virgo
Neptune	SnR/MnR/MCR	09° 46' Cancer	15° 29' Pisces
Pluto	MCOvR	21° 45' Gemini	27° 28' Aquarius

SUE: born Greenock, Scotland; 0415 GMT, 18 June 1908

	Rulership	*Sign*	*Overlay*
Ascendant		04° 22' Cancer	00° 00' Aries
Descendent		04° 22' Capricorn	00° 00' Libra
Midheaven		22° 39' Aquarius	18° 17' Scorpio
Nadir		22° 39' Leo	18° 17' Taurus
Sun	ICR	26° 25' Gemini	22° 02' Pisces
Moon	ChR	15° 41' Aquarius	11° 19' Scorpio
Mercury	SnR	17° 08' Cancer	12° 46' Aries
Venus	ICOvR	21° 36' Cancer	17° 14' Aries
Mars		17° 07' Cancer	12° 25' Aries
Jupiter		11° 55' Leo	07° 33' Taurus
Saturn	DecR	09° 12' Aries	04° 50' Capricorn
Uranus	MnR/MCR	20° 02' Capricorn	15° 40' Libra
Neptune	SnOvR	13° 53' Cancer	09° 32' Aries
Pluto	MCOvR/ MnOvR	24° 21' Gemini	19° 59' Pisces

KIT: born Greenock, Scotland; 1630 GMT, 8 August 1909

	Rulership	*Sign*	*Overlay*
Ascendant		13° 07' Sagittarius	00° 00' Aries
Descendent		13° 07' Gemini	00° 00' Libra
Midheaven		20° 49' Libra	07° 42' Aquarius
Nadir		20° 49' Aries	07° 42' Leo
Sun	SnR/ICOvR	15° 26' Leo	02° 19' Sagittarius
Moon		17° 58' Taurus	04° 51' Virgo
Mercury	DecR/MnOvR	19° 56' Leo	06° 49' Sagittarius
Venus	MnR/MCR	12° 58' Virgo	29° 31' Sagittarius
Mars	ICR	05° 00' Aries	21° 53' Cancer
Jupiter	ChR/SnOvR	18° 13' Virgo	05° 06' Capricorn
Saturn		23° 13' Aries	10° 06' Leo
Uranus	MCOvR	17° 59' Capricorn	04° 52' Taurus
Neptune		17° 50' Cancer	04° 42' Scorpio
Pluto		26° 28' Gemini	13° 21' Libra

JIM A.: born Greenock, Scotland; 1945 GMT, 22 November 1910

	Rulership	Sign	Overlay
Ascendant		25° 20′ Cancer	00° 00′ Aries
Descendent		25° 20′ Capricorn	00° 00′ Libra
Midheaven		21° 51′ Pisces	26° 31′ Scorpio
Nadir		21° 51′ Virgo	26° 31′ Taurus
Sun	MnR/SnOvR	29° 38′ Scorpio	04° 18′ Leo
Moon	ChR	18° 13′ Leo	22° 53′ Aries
Mercury	ICR	04° 01′ Sagittarius	08° 41′ Leo
Venus	ICOvR	28° 44′ Scorpio	03° 24′ Leo
Mars	MnOvR	10° 58′ Scorpio	15° 38′ Cancer
Jupiter		02° 19′ Scorpio	06° 59′ Cancer
Saturn	DecR	01° 59′ Taurus	06° 39′ Capricorn
Uranus		22° 24′ Capricorn	27° 04′ Virgo
Neptune	MCR	21° 23′ Cancer	26° 03′ Pisces
Pluto	SnR/MCOvR	27° 26′ Gemini	02° 06′ Pisces

MARGARET: born Greenock, Scotland; 0615 GMT,
7 September 1914

	Rulership	Sign	Overlay
Ascendant		19° 43′ Virgo	00° 00′ Aries
Descendent		19° 43′ Pisces	00° 00′ Libra
Midheaven		15° 44′ Gemini	26° 01° Sagittarius
Nadir		15° 44′ Sagittarius	26° 01′ Gemini
Sun		13° 46′ Virgo	24° 03′ Pisces
Moon		13° 40′ Aries	23° 57′ Libra
Mercury	ChR/SnR/MCR/ ICOvR	20° 32′ Virgo	00° 49′ Aries
Venus	MnOvR	29° 39′ Libra	09° 56′ Taurus
Mars	MnR	15° 14′ Libra	25° 31′ Aries
Jupiter	ICR/MCOvR	14° 06′ Aquarius	24° 23′ Leo
Saturn		01° 01′ Cancer	11° 18′ Capricorn
Uranus		08° 22′ Aquarius	18° 39′ Leo
Neptune	DecR/SnOvR	29° 35′ Cancer	09° 52′ Aquarius
Pluto		02° 06′ Cancer	12° 23′ Capricorn

ALICE: born Bradford, England; 1000 GMT, 30 January 1921

	Rulership	Sign	Overlay
Ascendant		19° 00′ Aries	00° 00′ Aries
Descendent		19° 00′ Libra	00° 00′ Libra
Midheaven		06° 39′ Capricorn	17° 39′ Sagittarius
Nadir		06° 39′ Cancer	17° 39′ Gemini
Sun		10° 00′ Aquarius	21° 00′ Capricorn
Moon	ICR	05° 05′ Scorpio	16° 05′ Libra
Mercury	ICOvR	21° 16′ Aquarius	02° 16′ Aquarius
Venus	MnOvR/DecR	26° 25′ Pisces	07° 25′ Pisces
Mars	ChR	19° 25′ Pisces	00° 25′ Pisces
Jupiter	MCOvR	17° 50′ Scorpio	28° 50′ Libra
Saturn	SnOvR/MCR	24° 13′ Virgo	05° 13′ Virgo
Uranus	SnR	04° 08′ Pisces	15° 08′ Aquarius
Neptune		12° 27′ Leo	23° 27′ Cancer
Pluto	MnR	07° 16′ Cancer	18° 16′ Gemini

Second Generation's Partners (and in-laws where known)
Sue's husband, GERARD: born Bradford, England; 'early morning'
rectified to 0510 GMT, 2 June 1914

	Rulership	Sign	Overlay
Ascendant		02° 10′ Cancer	00° 00′ Aries
Descendent		02° 10′ Capricorn	00° 00′ Libra
Midheaven		23° 10′ Aquarius	21° 00′ Scorpio
Nadir		23° 10′ Leo	21° 00′ Taurus
Sun	ICR	10° 48′ Gemini	08° 38′ Pisces
Moon	ChR	18° 51′ Virgo	16° 41′ Gemini
Mercury	SnR/MnR/ MnOvR	28° 07′ Gemini	25° 57′ Pisces
Venus	ICOvR	08° 25′ Cancer	06° 15′ Aries
Mars		16° 25′ Leo	14° 15′ Taurus
Jupiter		22° 09′ Aquarius	19° 59′ Scorpio
Saturn	DecR	20° 12′ Gemini	18° 02′ Pisces
Uranus	MCR	11° 31′ Aquarius	09° 21′ Scorpio
Neptune	SnOvR	26° 16′ Cancer	24° 06′ Aries
Pluto	MCOvR	00° 09′ Cancer	27° 59′ Pisces

Margaret's husband, BERT: born Bradford, England;
6 October 1920 (time unknown)

	Rulership	Sign	Overlay
Ascendant			
Descendent			
Midheaven			
Nadir			
Sun	MnR?	13° 00' Libra approximately	
Moon	MnR?	25° 00' Cancer to 09° 00' Leo approximately	
Mercury		01° 00' Scorpio approximately	
Venus	SnR	08° 00' Scorpio approximately	
Mars		21° 00' Sagittarius approximately	
Jupiter		08° 00' Virgo approximately	
Saturn		18° 00' Virgo approximately	
Uranus		02° 00' Pisces approximately	
Neptune		13° 00' Leo approximately	
Pluto		08° 00' Cancer approximately	

Alice's husband, JOHN D: born Bradford, England;
1 June 1915 (time unknown)

	Rulership	Sign	Overlay
Ascendant			
Descendent			
Midheaven			
Nadir			
Sun		10° 00' Gemini approximately	
Moon		23° 00' Capricorn to 07° 00' Aquarius approximately	
Mercury	SnR	03° 00' Cancer approximately	
Venus		12° 00' Taurus approximately	
Mars		04° 00' Taurus approximately	
Jupiter		25° 00' Pisces approximately	
Saturn	MnR?	06° 00' Cancer approximately	
Uranus	MnR?	15° 00' Aquarius approximately	
Neptune		29° 00' Cancer	
Pluto		01° 00' Cancer approximately	

Sue's mother-in-law, SARAH: born Castle Gresley, England;
25 April 1875 (time unknown)

	Rulership	*Sign*	*Overlay*
Ascendant			
Descendent			
Midheaven			
Nadir			
Sun		05° 00′ Taurus approximately	
Moon		23° 00′ Virgo to 07° 00′ Libra approximately	
Mercury	MnR?	21° 00′ Aries approximately	
Venus	MnR? SnR	05° 00′ Aries approximately	
Mars		01° 00′ Capricorn approximately	
Jupiter		25° 00′ Libra approximately	
Saturn		24° 00′ Aquarius approximately	
Uranus		11° 00′ Leo approximately	
Neptune		00° 00′ Taurus approximately	
Pluto		? Taurus approximately	

Sue's father-in-law, PATSY: born Bradford, England;
27 July 1867 (time unknown)

	Rulership	*Sign*	*Overlay*
Ascendant			
Descendent			
Midheaven			
Nadir			
Sun	SnR	05° 00′ Leo approximately	
Moon		25° 00′ Taurus to 09° 00′ Gemini approximately	
Mercury	MnR?	21° 00′ Cancer approximately	
Venus	MnR?	16° 00′ Taurus approximately	
Mars		23° 00′ Virgo approximately	
Jupiter		06° 00′ Pisces approximately	
Saturn		17° 00′ Scorpio approximately	
Uranus		10° 00′ Cancer approximately	
Neptune		15° 00′ Taurus approximately	
Pluto		? Taurus approximately	

The Third Generation

ROSEMARY (Sue's daugher): born Bradford, England;
0120 GMT (0320 DST), 16 May 1942

	Rulership	*Sign*	*Overlay*
Ascendant		15° 48′ Aquarius	00° 00′ Aries
Descendent		15° 48′ Leo	00° 00′ Libra
Midheaven		12° 56′ Sagittarius	27° 08′ Capricorn
Nadir		12° 56′ Gemini	27° 08′ Cancer
Sun	DecR	24° 33′ Taurus	08° 45′ Cancer
Moon	SnOvR/MnOvR/ ICOvR	03° 32′ Gemini	17° 44′ Cancer
Mercury	MnR/ICR	16° 18′ Gemini	00° 30′ Leo
Venus	SnR	10° 54′ Aries	25° 06′ Taurus
Mars		12° 06′ Cancer	26° 18′ Leo
Jupiter	MCR	24° 23′ Gemini	08° 35′ Leo
Saturn	MCOvR	00° 55′ Gemini	15° 07′ Cancer
Uranus	ChR	00° 03′ Gemini	14° 15′ Cancer
Neptune		27° 15′ Virgo	11° 27′ Scorpio
Pluto		03° 40′ Leo	17° 52′ Virgo

BARBARA (Alice's daugher): born Bradford, England;
1930 GMT, 5 March 1948

	Rulership	*Sign*	*Overlay*
Ascendant		18° 08′ Scorpio	00° 00′ Aries
Descendent		18° 08′ Taurus	00° 00′ Libra
Midheaven		09° 10′ Virgo	21° 02′ Aquarius
Nadir		09° 10′ Pisces	27° 01′ Cancer
Sun	ICOvR	15° 09′ Pisces	27° 01′ Cancer
Moon	SnOvR	13° 46′ Capricorn	25° 38′ Taurus
Mercury	MCR	21° 39′ Aquarius	03° 31′ Cancer
Venus	DecR/MnOvR	26° 35′ Aries	08° 27′ Virgo
Mars		21° 51′ Leo	03° 43′ Capricorn
Jupiter		26° 25′ Sagittarius	08° 17′ Taurus
Saturn	MnR	17° 19′ Leo	29° 11′ Sagittarius
Uranus	MCOvR	22° 08′ Gemini	04° 00′ Scorpio
Neptune	SnR/ICR	12° 22′ Libra	24° 14′ Aquarius
Pluto	ChR	13° 06′ Leo	24° 58′ Sagittarius

JANET (Margaret's daughter): born Bradford, England; 0000 GMT (0100 BST), 17 July 1954

	Rulership	Sign	Overlay
Ascendant		21° 33′ Taurus	00° 00′ Aries
Descendent		21° 33′ Scorpio	00° 00′ Libra
Midheaven		20° 49′ Capricorn	29° 16′ Scorpio
Nadir		20° 49′ Cancer	29° 16′ Taurus
Sun		23° 53′ Cancer	02° 20′ Gemini
Moon	SnR/ICR	05° 53′ Aquarius	14° 20′ Sagittarius
Mercury	SnOvR	09° 17′ Cancer	17° 44′ Taurus
Venus	ChR/ICOvR	04° 11′ Virgo	12° 38′ Cancer
Mars		26° 42′ Sagittarius	05° 09′ Scorpio
Jupiter	MnOvR	12° 03′ Cancer	20° 30′ Taurus
Saturn	MCR	02° 44′ Scorpio	11° 11′ Virgo
Uranus	MnR	23° 24′ Cancer	01° 51′ Gemini
Neptune		23° 19′ Libra	01° 46′ Virgo
Pluto	DecR/MCOvR	23° 49′ Leo	02° 16′ Cancer

TONY (Margaret's son): born Bradford, England; 1630 GMT (1730 BST), 8 September 1955

	Rulership	Sign	Overlay
Ascendant		16° 50′ Capricorn	00° 00′ Aries
Descendent		16° 50′ Cancer	00° 00′ Libra
Midheaven		24° 51′ Scorpio	08° 01′ Aquarius
Nadir		24° 51′ Taurus	08° 01′ Leo
Sun	MnOvR/ICOvR	15° 15′ Virgo	28° 25′ Scorpio
Moon	DecR	06° 46′ Gemini	19° 56′ Leo
Mercury	SnR/MnR	09° 56′ Libra	23° 06′ Sagittarius
Venus	ICR	17° 15′ Scorpio	00° 25′ Aquarius
Mars		07° 48′ Virgo	20° 58′ Scorpio
Jupiter		18° 44′ Leo	01° 54′ Scorpio
Saturn	ChR	16° 34′ Scorpio	29° 44′ Capricorn
Uranus	MCOvR	00° 28′ Leo	13° 38′ Libra
Neptune		26° 28′ Libra	09° 38′ Capricorn
Pluto	MCR/SnOvR	27° 05′ Leo	10° 15′ Scorpio

RICHARD (Alice's son): born Bradford, England;
1245 GMT (1345 BST) 13 July 1960

	Rulership	Sign	Overlay
Ascendant		20° 59' Libra	00° 00' Aries
Descendent		20° 59' Aries	00° 00' Libra
Midheaven		28° 38' Cancer	07° 39' Capricorn
Nadir		28° 38' Capricorn	07° 39' Cancer
Sun		21° 06' Cancer	00° 07' Capricorn
Moon	SnR/MCR/ ICOvR	25° 14' Pisces	04° 15' Virgo
Mercury	MnOvR	26° 43' Cancer	05° 44' Capricorn
Venus	ChR	26° 52' Cancer	05° 53' Capricorn
Mars	DecR	16° 34' Taurus	25° 35' Libra
Jupiter		25° 55' Sagittarius	04° 56' Gemini
Saturn	ICR/SnOvR/ McOvR	14° 40' Capricorn	23° 41' Gemini
Uranus		19° 31' Leo	28° 32' Capricorn
Neptune	Mnr	06° 22' Scorpio	15° 23' Aries
Pluto		04° 26' Virgo	13° 27' Aquarius

Third Generation's Partners (and in-laws, where known)
Rosemary's husband, HARRY S: born Bradford, England;
1800 GMT (1900 BST) 1 May 1937

	Rulership	Sign	Overlay
Ascendant		25° 35' Libra	00° 00' Aries
Descendent		25° 35' Aries	00° 00' Libra
Midheaven		05° 09' Leo	09° 34' Capricorn
Nadir		05° 09' Aquarius	09° 34' Cancer
Sun	MCR	10° 02' Taurus	14° 27' Libra
Moon	ICOvR	17° 37' Capricorn	22° 02' Gemini
Mercury	MnOvR	24° 20' Taurus	25° 45' Libra
Venus	ChR/SnR/ SnOvR	20° 35' Aries	25° 00' Virgo
Mars	DecR	03° 42' Sagittarius	08° 07' Taurus
Jupiter		27° 37' Capricorn	01° 02' Cancer
Saturn	MnR/MCOvR	00° 40' Aries	05° 05' Virgo
Uranus	ICR	09° 37' Taurus	14° 02' Libra
Neptune		16° 21' Virgo	20° 46' Aquarius
Pluto		26° 36' Cancer	01° 01' Capricorn

Barbara's husband, ANDREW: born London, England;
0400 GMT (0500 BST), 16 May 1951

	Rulership	Sign	Overlay
Ascendant		10° 39' Taurus	00° 00' Aries
Descendent		10° 39' Scorpio	00° 00' Libra
Midheaven		17° 04' Capricorn	06° 25' Sagittarius
Nadir		17° 04' Cancer	06° 25' Gemini
Sun	MnOvR	24° 30' Taurus	13° 31' Aries
Moon	ICR	17° 14' Virgo	06° 25' Leo
Mercury	MnR/ICOvR	00° 37' Taurus	19° 58' Pisces
Venus	ChR/SnR	05° 47' Cancer	25° 08' Taurus
Mars	SnOvR	26° 06' Taurus	15° 27' Aries
Jupiter	McOvR	05° 12' Aries	24° 33' Aquarius
Saturn	MCR	25° 39' Virgo	15° 00' Leo
Uranus		07° 06' Cancer	26° 27' Taurus
Neptune		17° 14' Libra	06° 35' Virgo
Pluto	DecR	17° 29' Leo	06° 50' Cancer

Janet's husband, JUAN: born Guadalajara, Mexico;
1000 GMT (1600 local time), 24 December 1954

	Rulership	Sign	Overlay
Ascendant		14° 24' Scorpio	00° 00' Aries
Descendent		14° 24' Taurus	00° 00' Libra
Midheaven		15° 32' Leo	01° 08' Capricorn
Nadir		15° 32' Aquarius	01° 08' Cancer
Sun		02° 59' Capricorn	15° 02' Taurus
Moon	ICOvR	02° 28' Libra	18° 04' Aquarius
Mercury		22° 22' Capricorn	07° 58' Gemini
Venus	MnR/DecR/ SnOvR	05° 45' Sagittarius	21° 21' Aries
Mars		09° 26' Aries	25° 02' Leo
Jupiter		00° 59' Libra	16° 35' Aquarius
Saturn	SnR/MCOvR	08° 28' Sagittarius	24° 04' Aries
Uranus	ICR/MnOvR	06° 00' Leo	21° 36' Sagittarius
Neptune		02° 08' Scorpio	17° 44' Pisces
Pluto	ChR	00° 21' Virgo	15° 57' Capricorn

Rosemary's mother-in-law, MAUD: born Bradford,
'around tea-time' (rectified to 1600 GMT), 15 August 1911

	Rulership	Sign	Overlay
Ascendant		28° 01′ Sagittarius	00° 00′ Aries
Descendent		28° 01′ Gemini	00° 00′ Libra
Midheaven		24° 02′ Libra	26° 01′ Capricorn
Nadir		24° 02′ Aries	26° 01′ Cancer
Sun	SnR/MnOvR	21° 41′ Leo	23° 40′ Scorpio
Moon	ICOvR	28° 14′ Aries	00° 13′ Leo
Mercury	DecR	18° 54′ Virgo	20° 53′ Sagittarius
Venus	ICR	27° 48′ Virgo	29° 47′ Sagittarius
Mars	MnR/ICR	19° 14′ Taurus	21° 13′ Leo
Jupiter	ChR	07° 24′ Scorpio	09° 23′ Aquarius
Saturn	MCOvR	19° 55° Taurus	21° 54′ Leo
Uranus		26° 26′ Capricorn	28° 25′ Aries
Neptune		22° 34′ Cancer	24° 33′ Libra
Pluto	SnOvR	28° 38′ Gemini	00° 37′ Libra

Rosemary's father-in-law, HARRY W: born Bradford, England;
7 March 1913 (time unknown)

	Rulership	Sign	Overlay
Ascendant			
Descendent			
Midheaven			
Nadir			
Sun		16° 20′ Pisces approximately	
Moon		16° 00′ Pisces approximately	
Mercury		03° 46′ Aries approximately	
Venus		00° 36′ Taurus approximately	
Mars		12° 25′ Aquarius approximately	
Jupiter		12° 42′ Capricorn approximately	
Saturn		28° 27′ Taurus approximately	
Uranus		05° 51′ Aquarius approximately	
Neptune	SnR/MnR	23° 26′ Cancer approximately	
Pluto		28° 00′ Gemini approximately	

Barbara's mother-in-law, JOAN: born London, England;
1000 GMT (1100 BST), 2 August 1924

	Rulership	Sign	Overlay
Ascendant		07° 24′ Libra	00° 00′ Aries
Descendent		07° 24′ Aries	00° 00′ Libra
Midheaven		09° 39′ Cancer	02° 15′ Capricorn
Nadir		09° 39′ Capricorn	02° 15′ Cancer
Sun	SnR/MnR	09° 48′ Leo	02° 24′ Pisces
Moon	MCR/ICOvR	15° 44′ Leo	08° 20′ Pisces
Mercury		03° 58′ Virgo	26° 34′ Pisces
Venus	ChR	02° 58′ Cancer	25° 34′ Sagittarius
Mars	DecR	04° 30′ Pisces	27° 06′ Leo
Jupiter		10° 06′ Sagittarius	02° 42′ Gemini
Saturn	ICR/MCOvR	26° 35′ Libra	19° 09′ Aries
Uranus		20° 59′ Pisces	13° 35′ Virgo
Neptune	SnOvR/MnOvR	19° 43′ Leo	12° 19′ Pisces
Pluto		12° 37′ Cancer	05° 13′ Capricorn

Barbara's father-in-law, JOHN N: born London, England;
29 June 1923 (time unknown).

	Rulership	Sign	Overlay
Ascendant			
Descendent			
Midheaven			
Nadir			
Sun		06° 39′ Cancer approximately	
Moon	SnR	19° 12′ Capricorn approximately	
Mercury		15° 31′ Pisces approximately	
Venus		16° 59′ Gemini approximately	
Mars		19° 20′ Cancer approximately	
Jupiter		09° 09′ Scorpio approximately	
Saturn	MnR	13° 30′ Libra approximately	
Uranus		17° 33′ Pisces approximately	
Neptune		16° 20′ Leo approximately	
Pluto		10° 37′ Cancer approximately	

The Fourth Generation

HARRY A. (Rosemary's son): born Bradford, England;
0652 GMT (0752 BST) 7 September 1964

	Rulership	Sign	Overlay
Ascendant		28° 28' Virgo	00° 00' Aries
Descendent		28° 28' Pisces	00° 00' Libra
Midheaven		27° 56' Gemini	29° 28' Sagittarius
Nadir		27° 56' Sagittarius	29° 28' Gemini
Sun		14° 41' Virgo	16° 13' Pisces
Moon		28° 37' Virgo	00° 09' Aries
Mercury	ChR/SnR/MnR/ MCR/ICOvR	04° 43' Virgo	06° 15' Pisces
Venus		28° 57' Cancer	00° 29' Aquarius
Mars	MnOvR	25° 04' Cancer	26° 36' Capricorn
Jupiter	ICR/MCOvR	26° 01' Taurus	27° 33' Scorpio
Saturn		00° 40' Pisces	02° 12' Virgo
Uranus		10° 45' Virgo	12° 17' Pisces
Neptune	SnOvR/DecR	15° 32' Scorpio	17° 04' Taurus
Pluto		14° 01' Virgo	15° 33' Pisces

HELEN (Rosemary's daughter): born Bradford, England;
0520 GMT (0620 BST), 17 October 1969

	Rulership	Sign	Overlay
Ascendant		09° 24' Libra	00° 00' Aries
Descendent		09° 24' Aries	00° 00' Libra
Midheaven		12° 39' Cancer	03° 15' Capricorn
Nadir		12° 39' Capricorn	03° 15' Cancer
Sun		23° 40' Libra	14° 16' Aries
Moon	MCR/ICOvR	08° 43' Capricorn	29° 19' Gemini
Mercury	MnOvR	05° 57' Libra	26° 33' Pisces
Venus	ChR/SnR	29° 32' Virgo	20° 08' Pisces
Mars	DecR/SnOvR	16° 57' Capricorn	07° 33' Cancer
Jupiter		18° 00' Libra	08° 36' Aries
Saturn	MnR/ICR/ MCOvR	06° 24' Taurus	27° 00' Libra
Uranus		07° 20' Libra	27° 56' Pisces
Neptune		27° 12' Scorpio	17° 48' Taurus
Pluto		26° 58' Virgo	17° 34' Pisces

JENNY (Barbara's daughter): born Romford, England;
0200 GMT (0300 BST), 14 September 1976

	Rulership	Sign	Overlay
Ascendant		13° 55' Leo	00° 00' Aries
Descendent		13° 55' Aquarius	00° 00' Libra
Midheaven		25° 22' Aries	11° 57' Sagittarius
Nadir		25° 22' Libra	11° 57' Gemini
Sun	ChR	21° 23' Virgo	07° 58' Taurus
Moon		22° 21' Taurus	08° 56' Capricorn
Mercury	SnR/ICOvR	06° 22' Libra	22° 57' Taurus
Venus	MnR/ICR/ SnOvR	15° 05' Libra	01° 40' Gemini
Mars	MCR	13° 08' Libra	29° 43' Taurus
Jupiter	MCOvR	01° 08' Gemini	17° 43' Taurus
Saturn	MnOvR	12° 09' Leo	28° 44' Pisces
Uranus	DecR	08° 22' Scorpio	24° 57' Gemini
Neptune		11° 20' Sagittarius	27° 55' Cancer
Pluto		11° 01' Libra	27° 36' Taurus

ELIZABETH (Barbara's daughter): born Romford, England;
1530 GMT (1630 BST), 11 May 1979

	Rulership	Sign	Overlay
Ascendant		08° 06' Libra	00° 00' Aries
Descendent		08° 06' Aries	00° 00' Libra
Midheaven		10° 34' Cancer	02° 29' Capricorn
Nadir		10° 34' Capricorn	02° 29' Cancer
Sun		20° 20' Taurus	12° 15' Scorpio
Moon	MCR/ICOvR	14° 51' Scorpio	06° 46' Taurus
Mercury		01° 15' Taurus	23° 10' Libra
Venus	ChR/SnR/ MnOvR	22° 17' Aries	14° 12' Libra
Mars	DecR	28° 06' Aries	20° 01' Libra
Jupiter		02° 13' Leo	24° 08' Capricorn
Saturn	ICR/MCOvR	07° 05' Virgo	22° 00' Aquarius
Uranus		18° 55' Scorpio	10° 50' Taurus
Neptune		19° 54' Sagittarius	11° 49' Gemini
Pluto	MnR/SnOvR	16° 59' Libra	08° 54' Aries

JOHNNY (Janet's son): born Guadalajara, Mexico;
0615 GMT (1215 local time), 20 February 1982

	Rulership	Sign	Overlay
Ascendant		14° 51' Scorpio	00° 00' Aries
Descendent		14° 51' Taurus	00° 00' Libra
Midheaven		16° 02' Leo	01° 11' Capricorn
Nadir		16° 02' Aquarius	01° 11' Cancer
Sun	MCR/SnOvR	01° 16' Pisces	16° 25' Cancer
Moon	ICOvR	19° 27' Capricorn	04° 36' Gemini
Mercury	MnOvR	06° 53' Aquarius	22° 02' Gemini
Venus	DecR	22° 11' Aquarius	07° 20' Cancer
Mars		19° 10' Libra	04° 19' Pisces
Jupiter		09° 03' Sagittarius	24° 12' Aries
Saturn	MnR/MCOvR	08° 40' Libra	23° 49' Aquarius
Uranus	ICR	12° 50' Scorpio	27° 59' Pisces
Neptune	SnR	26° 40' Sagittarius	11° 49' Taurus
Pluto	ChR	29° 23' Libra	14° 32' Pisces

KATY (Janet's daughter): born Toulouse, France;
0945 GMT (1045 local time), 7 June 1984

	Rulership	Sign	Overlay
Ascendant		24° 20' Leo	00° 00' Aries
Descendent		24° 20' Aquarius	00° 00' Libra
Midheaven		15° 58' Taurus	21° 38' Sagittarius
Nadir		15° 58' Scorpio	21° 38' Gemini
Sun	ChR	16° 49' Gemini	22° 29' Capricorn
Moon		26° 15' Virgo	01° 55' Taurus
Mercury	SnR/MnR/ ICOvR	29° 34' Taurus	05° 14' Capricorn
Venus	MCR/MnOvR	14° 30' Pisces	20° 10' Libra
Mars		12° 45' Scorpio	18° 25' Gemini
Jupiter	MCOvR	10° 45' Capricorn	16° 25' Leo
Saturn	SnOvR	10° 40' Scorpio	16° 20' Gemini
Uranus	DecR	11° 21' Sagittarius	17° 01' Cancer
Neptune		00° 26' Capricorn	06° 06' Leo
Pluto	ICR	29° 36' Libra	05° 16' Gemini

Fourth Generation Partners and in-laws (where known)

Harry A.'s fiancé, WENDY: born Maidstone, England;
8 October 1965 (time unknown)

	Rulership	Sign	Overlay
Ascendant			
Descendent			
Midheaven			
Nadir			
Sun		15° 00′ Libra approximately	
Moon		21° 00′ Pisces approximately	
Mercury		23° 00′ Libra approximately	
Venus	SnR	28° 00′ Scorpio approximately	
Mars		03° 00′ Sagittarius approximately	
Jupiter		01° 00′ Cancer approximately	
Saturn		11° 00′ Pisces approximately	
Uranus		17° 00′ Virgo approximately	
Neptune	MnR	18° 00′ Scorpio approximately	
Pluto		17° 00′ Virgo approximately	

Harry A.'s wife, KAREN: born Bradford, England;
0045 BST, 21 May 1968

	Rulership	Sign	Overlay
Ascendant		17° 44′ Capricorn	00° 00′ Aries
Descendent		17° 44′ Cancer	00° 00′ Libra
Midheaven		25° 35′ Scorpio	07° 51′ Aquarius
Nadir		25° 35′ Taurus	07° 51′ Leo
Sun	SnOvR/ICOvR	29° 59′ Taurus	12° 15′ Leo
Moon	DecR	20° 31′ Pisces	02° 04′ Gemini
Mercury	MnOvR	21° 45′ Gemini	04° 01′ Virgo
Venus	SnR/ICR	21° 45′ Taurus	04° 01′ Leo
Mars		08° 40′ Gemini	20° 56′ Leo
Jupiter		27° 05′ Leo	09° 21′ Scorpio
Saturn	ChR	20° 52′ Aries	03° 08′ Cancer
Uranus	MCOvR	25° 09′ Virgo	07° 25′ Sagittarius
Neptune	MnR	25° 04′ Scorpio	07° 20′ Aquarius
Pluto	MCR	20° 12′ Virgo	02° 28′ Sagittarius

Helen's husband, DAVID: born Morecambe, England;
1015 GMT, 13 January 1967

	Rulership	Sign	Overlay
Ascendant		14° 02' Pisces	00° 00' Aries
Descendent		14° 02' Virgo	00° 00' Libra
Midheaven		23° 48' Sagittarius	09° 46' Capricorn
Nadir		23° 48' Gemini	09° 46' Cancer
Sun		22° 32' Capricorn	08° 30' Aquarius
Moon	ICOvR	23° 35' Aquarius	09° 33' Pisces
Mercury	ICR/DecR	19° 37' Capricorn	05° 35' Aquarius
Venus		08° 17' Aquarius	24° 15' Aquarius
Mars		19° 40' Libra	05° 38' Scorpio
Jupiter	MCR	00° 22' Leo	16° 20' Leo
Saturn	SnR/MCOvR	24° 53' Pisces	10° 51' Aries
Uranus	MnR/SnOvR	24° 19' Virgo	10° 17' Libra
Neptune	ChR/MnOvR	23° 54' Scorpio	09° 49' Sagittarius
Pluto		20° 31' Virgo	06° 29' Libra

Harry A.'s mother-in-law, LINDA: born Bradford, England;
0800 GMT (0900 BST), 15 September 1951

	Rulership	Sign	Overlay
Ascendant		18° 50' Pisces	00° 00' Aries
Descendent		18° 50' Virgo	00° 00' Libra
Midheaven		26° 09' Sagittarius	07° 19' Capricorn
Nadir		26° 09' Sagittarius	07° 19' Capricorn
Sun		22° 05' Virgo	03° 15' Libra
Moon	ICOvR	24° 41' Pisces	05° 51' Aries
Mercury	SnR/DecR/ICR	04° 18' Scorpio	15° 28' Scorpio
Venus	SnOvR	03° 52' Virgo	15° 02' Virgo
Mars	MnOvR	18° 01' Leo	29° 11' Leo
Jupiter	MCR	11° 24' Aries	22° 34' Aries
Saturn	MCOvR	03° 48' Libra	14° 58' Aries
Uranus		13° 27' Cancer	24° 37' Cancer
Neptune	ChR/MnR	18° 17' Libra	29° 27' Libra
Pluto		20° 29' Leo	01° 39' Virgo

Harry A.'s father-in-law, MICK: born Bradford, England;
18 November 1946 (time unknown)

	Rulership	Sign	Overlay
Ascendant			
Descendent			
Midheaven			
Nadir			
Sun		26° 00' Scorpio approximately	
Moon		17° 00' Gemini approximately	
Mercury	MnR	12° 00' Scorpio approximately	
Venus		21° 00' Libra approximately	
Mars		24° 00' Sagittarius approximately	
Jupiter		00° 00' Capricorn approximately	
Saturn		05° 00' Virgo approximately	
Uranus		29° 00' Gemini approximately	
Neptune		14° 00' Libra approximately	
Pluto	SnR	16° 00' Leo approximately	

Helen's mother-in-law, DOREEN: born Bradford, England;
1605 GMT (1805 DST), 2 May 1944

	Rulership	Sign	Overlay
Ascendant		04° 25' Libra	00° 00' Aries
Descendent		04° 25' Aries	00° 00' Libra
Midheaven		09° 11' Cancer	04° 46' Capricorn
Nadir		09° 11' Capricorn	04° 46' Cancer
Sun		12° 07' Taurus	07° 42' Scorpio
Moon	MCR/ICOvR	08° 23' Virgo	03° 58' Pisces
Mercury	MnR	12° 10' Taurus	07° 45' Scorpio
Venus	ChR/SnR	12° 08' Aries	07° 43' Libra
Mars	DecR	24° 16' Cancer	19° 51' Capricorn
Jupiter		25° 28' Leo	21° 03' Aquarius
Saturn	ICR/MCOvR	24° 16' Gemini	19° 51' Sagittarius
Uranus		07° 20' Gemini	02° 55' Sagittarius
Neptune	MnOvR	01° 55' Libra	27° 30' Pisces
Pluto	SnOvR	06° 27' Leo	02° 02' Aquarius

Helen's father-in-law WILF: born Bradford, England;
0410 GMT (0510 BST), 13 January 1941

	Rulership	Sign	Overlay
Ascendant		24° 50′ Scorpio	00° 00′ Aries
Descendent		24° 50′ Taurus	00° 00′ Libra
Midheaven		19° 40′ Virgo	24° 01′ Capricorn
Nadir		19° 40′ Pisces	24° 01′ Cancer
Sun		22° 36′ Capricorn	27° 46′ Taurus
Moon	MnR/ICOvR	19° 03′ Cancer	24° 13′ Scorpio
Mercury	MCR	23° 43′ Capricorn	28° 53′ Taurus
Venus	DecR/SnOvR	29° 06′ Sagittarius	04° 16′ Taurus
Mars		05° 38′ Sagittarius	10° 48′ Aries
Jupiter		05° 59′ Taurus	11° 09′ Virgo
Saturn	SnR	07° 54′ Taurus	13° 04′ Virgo
Uranus		22° 16′ Taurus	13° 04′ Virgo
Neptune	ICR	25° 26′ Virgo	00° 36′ Aquarius
Pluto	ChR/MnOvR	03° 25′ Leo	08° 35′ Sagittarius

Fifth Generation

RICHARD A: born Maidstone, England;
1542 GMT, 25 January 1986

	Rulership	Sign	Overlay
Ascendant		28° 13′ Cancer	00° 00′ Aries
Descendent		28° 13′ Capricorn	00° 00′ Libra
Midheaven		29° 43′ Pisces	03° 30′ Sagittarius
Nadir		29° 43′ Virgo	03° 30′ Gemini
Sun	MnR	05° 23′ Aquarius	09° 10′ Libra
Moon	ChR	01° 03′ Leo	04° 50′ Aries
Mercury	ICR/ICOvR	01° 03′ Pisces	04° 50′ Scorpio
Venus	SnOvR	06° 48′ Aquarius	10° 35′ Libra
Mars	MnOvR	25° 28′ Scorpio	29° 15′ Cancer
Jupiter	MCOvR	23° 48′ Aquarius	27° 35′ Libra
Saturn	DecR	07° 28′ Sagittarius	11° 15′ Leo
Uranus	SnR	20° 49′ Sagittarius	24° 36′ Leo
Neptune	MCR	04° 29′ Capricorn	08° 16′ Virgo
Pluto		07° 18′ Scorpio	11° 05′ Cancer

This completes the family to date.

Index

✦ Aries

✦ Taurus

✦ Gemini

♋ Cancer

♌ Leo

♍ Virgo

♎ Libra

♏ Scorpio

♐ Sagittarius

♑ Capricorn

♒ Aquarius

♓ Pisces